GOD BLESS THIS
Mess

GOD BLESS THIS
Mess

LEARNING TO LIVE AND LOVE THROUGH
LIFE'S BEST (AND WORST) MOMENTS

HANNAH BROWN

with **MARK DAGOSTINO**

HARPER

An Imprint of HarperCollins*Publishers*

Some names in this book have been changed to protect the privacy of others who, unlike me, didn't choose to share their hearts and histories on television.

GOD BLESS THIS MESS. Copyright © 2021 by Hannah Kelsey Brown. All rights reserved. Printed in the United States of America. No part of this book may be used or reproduced in any manner whatsoever without written permission except in the case of brief quotations embodied in critical articles and reviews. For information, address HarperCollins Publishers, 195 Broadway, New York, NY 10007.

HarperCollins books may be purchased for educational, business, or sales promotional use. For information, please email the Special Markets Department at SPsales@harpercollins.com.

FIRST EDITION

Designed by Nancy Singer

Interior art: iStock/Iuliia_Zubkova.

Insert art: photo frame on pages 1–6, 8–10, 13–16 @32 pixels/stock. adobe.com; torn paper on pages 7, 15 @ yulliash/stock.adobe.com; pink background on pages 1–16 @Unchalee/stock.adobe.com; pink background texture on pages 5, 9, 11, 12 @reconceptus/stock.adobe.com.

Library of Congress Cataloging-in-Publication Data has been applied for.

ISBN 978-0-06-309820-6

21 22 23 24 25   LSC   10 9 8 7 6 5 4 3 2 1

To those in the middle of the mess . . .

Contents

GOD BLESS THIS
Mess

Introduction

I'm a total train wreck."

That's a pretty big thing to admit, let alone to say to another person. Let alone to say to a stranger. And when I said it back in early 2018, I wasn't talking to myself in the mirror at the end of a really hard day. I didn't write it in my journal. I didn't say it to my therapist or a close girlfriend. I wasn't even talking to my mom.

I said it to a camera crew—in front of millions of viewers on TV.

Then I took things one step further: "The hot-mess express," I said, when they asked me to sum up my life. "And I'm the conductor! *Toot-toot!*"

Can you imagine? This was my chance to introduce myself to the potential man of my dreams (not to mention a worldwide television audience) when I went on a little show called *The Bachelor*, and *those* were the words I chose to describe myself.

I'll tell you what, though: I wasn't lying. I think a lot of people who've watched me on TV or followed me on Instagram would say I have lived up to that description to a T.

And I'm okay with that.

I *am* a hot mess.

I don't mean it in a negative way. It's just the truth. I'm twenty-six years old as I'm writing this book. I'm smack in the middle of trying to figure out who I am as a person. Lots of girls go through big changes and tough relationships and crazy challenges as they transition from teens and young women into full-blown adults. I'm not alone, right? (*Please, God, tell me I'm not alone!*)

At times I feel like I'm going through some sort of quarter-life crisis. Is that even a thing? If not, then I think we should make it a thing, because lots of people I know seem to be going through something similar.

The only difference is, I've been doing it while millions of people are watching.

While this is not a *Bachelor* or *Bachelorette* book, my time on those shows, followed by my winning season on *Dancing with the Stars*, just happened to come when I was going through some of the biggest changes and most challenging struggles of my life. I was watched, loved, hated, admired, scolded, and scorned, all at once, in public, while all kinds of commentators kept talking about my struggles with faith and sex and feminism in front of the whole world, in women's magazines, on competing TV networks, and even on NPR. And that led me to develop an audience of millions of fans of my own on social media; followers who tell me all the time that they're just so happy to see someone be real on TV; happy to see someone who wears her heart on her sleeve; someone who reminds them a little bit of themselves and what their lives would be like if the cameras captured their reality on TV, messes and all. Mostly, they tell me how refreshing it is to see someone who's so open, which has made me feel empowered to open up even more.

But guess what? My most private thoughts, my private moments, the emotional history that led me to become the mess I became, have all been kept safe in my heart and in my journals. I've never shared the stuff that I hope is most relatable to you, the person who's holding this book. Until now.

There were nights when my smiling face was out there drawing big ratings for these popular TV shows when in real life I was sitting alone in an empty apartment, eating takeout food with a plastic fork, crying my eyes out, wiping snot from my face, and questioning why God was testing me like this. Why was I feeling so inadequate, not trusting my gut, chasing false trophies, allowing myself to be betrayed by men who said they loved me, not recognizing the difference between real love and something less? Why was I so afraid to express my true thoughts and feelings, not only with men but in so many aspects of my life?

Maybe it's because sometimes I didn't even know or understand what my own true thoughts and feelings were.

My life really was a complete mess, and God bless all of it. Because it's in the messes where we learn the most—as long as we slow down enough to realize what God is trying to show us.

For most of my life the idea of slowing down had been a problem for me, but by early 2020 it was full-on out of control. It felt like my "hot-mess express" was going two hundred miles per hour when the pandemic stood up and pulled on the emergency brake. And then, just like everybody else, I found myself facing the world at a standstill.

All of a sudden I had time on my hands. For the first time since I can't even remember, I stopped moving from one thing to the next and the next and the next. And whether I wanted to or not, whether I was ready for it or not, whether I liked it or not, the quarantine (and a couple of mistakes I made during that time) forced me to take a good long look in the mirror.

That's a *good* thing. I mean, it should be, right? How often do we get a chance to stop and really think about what we're doing, who we are, and who we want to be? With 100 percent of my new career opportunities in Hollywood on hold for a moment, I finally got a chance to ask myself why I was going so fast in the first place—and why that felt so important.

The thing is, when you live so much life so quickly, you *change*. That's not a bad thing, but I realized that whenever someone asked me to explain my experience over the past few years, or even over the past several months, I actually had a visceral reaction. I would take a big gulp, heave an even bigger sigh, and immediately feel my throat close up to prevent the words from coming out. It's like every thought would leave my mind, and I wanted to flee the conversation. I was paralyzed by the wave of emotions that rushed over my body in a matter of seconds.

Why is that?

Maybe it *is* because I've lived so much life so quickly. It feels like I've done fifteen years' worth of living since 2018. I've gone from being a private person, living in small-town Alabama, to being known all over the world. And *flying* all over the world. I had never even left the country before. I've gone from single to engaged to single again. I've dated more men than some women do in a lifetime. I slept with more men in one week than I'd slept with in my entire life. And I've gone from losing touch with my faith to coming back around to find Jesus still loves me, through all of my mistakes, my suffering, my losses, my wins, and everything in between.

Taking the time to try and find answers for myself has been one of those hurts-so-good things. You know what I'm talking about?

The first thing that comes to mind when I think of a hurts-so-good experience—okay, well, maybe the second (thank you, John Mellencamp)—is a deep-tissue massage. Like, super painful and torturous in the moment. You think about turning over and punching the masseuse when she puts her entire body weight on the knot you worked really hard to get from all the stress you figuratively, and now literally, put on your shoulders. But after a few days the soreness goes away, the boulder knot of stress dissipates—for a little while, at least—and you feel better.

Well, that's what I want to do with this book: to give you a hurts-so-good experience that allows your own soreness and pain to go away for a while—and maybe make you feel a little bit better about yourself while we do it.

Since long before the quarantines started, I've been diving into self-help books by all sorts of authors, trying to find solace and answers to all my worries, or at least the feeling that someone out there gets what I'm going through. Here's what usually happens: I start reading the book in hopes of gaining some insight, I find a place where the author describes my feelings and experiences way better than I ever could, and then I'm like, "Gah, why can't I express myself so eloquently?" The struggle/experience/feeling resonates with me. But then it seems like the writer always finds a solution, and I realize I'm not quite *there* yet. I'm not at the solution stage. I'm still in the thick of it. I know from experience that when I try to handle things with the maturity of Brené Brown, Oprah Winfrey, Glennon Doyle, or anyone else who has lived so much more *life* than me, it doesn't work. I don't wind up getting the same results. So I close the book and think, *Oh, I wish I could be that wise!*

So many of these authors seem like they've found answers to life's questions. They've made it through the fire. They've tested their faith. They've come up with formulas and tricks and habits and routines that get them through anything, to the point where they come out on the other side shining like the powerful women they are.

Not me. Not yet. I feel like no matter how hard I try, life keeps kicking my butt and testing me again and again. Sometimes I wonder, is this ever gonna get any easier?

After months and months of spiritual reflection, spending dozens of hours in the comfort of good teachers and positive friends, shaking off some of the burdens I've been carrying since childhood through therapy and some long talks with my mom and dad, it's finally dawned on me: Maybe I was given this very public platform because *I'm* the one who needs to write the book. Maybe I need to share the stories I was looking so hard to find in all those books I read. Maybe God's answer to my question is that I'm supposed to share the hurt and the healing that I've been through during this crazy-intense portion of my life with others. Maybe talking about it and connecting with all of *you* is what will make it easier—not just for me, but for you, too.

I know the Lord didn't put me through so much public pain for no reason. I need to have a public healing, too. Maybe I've gone through all of this so I can be someone in the public eye that people can look to who *doesn't* have it all together yet—but who isn't totally falling apart either.

My hope is that *God Bless This Mess* will be the book I wish I'd had: a book that gives other girls just trying to figure out life an honest account of how beautiful messes can actually be. It's the story of what

I've gone through, what I'm going through, and how I'm working on it—with the comfort of knowing that, like other young women, I don't have all the answers. What I *do* have is experience. I've been through some seriously humbling, humiliating moments, both in private and in public. And there's something beautiful about that, once you've been humbled enough to see it from a new point of view. I've gotten stuck in so many storms with no umbrella, wearing white shoes, and I've grown stronger, more resilient, and better prepared for whatever life throws at me because of them.

Lysa TerKeurst, one of my favorite Christian writers, once wrote, "Wisdom is our silver lining. Wisdom will help us not repeat the mistakes we've made but rather grow stronger through them." Which means that our *best* worst mistakes are the ones that can teach us the most.

Here's the good thing about having lived what feels like fifteen years in three: I don't have to wait until I'm forty to write this book! The hurting and hell I've been through was all so I can share the healing with readers like you, right now, when I'm not yet married, I'm not a mom, I'm not living for another person or people. I'm living for me—and trying my best to live for the Lord.

We all long for connection, to feel seen and heard, wanted and understood. (That's part of the reason we're all living our lives out on social media, right?) We don't need to be fixed or given a how-to. What we really need is to be loved and accepted. And while I sometimes have a hard time believing anyone should look to me for a list of what to do and not to do in life, I do believe I'm a girl who can offer some comfort—a relatable voice to help others feel not alone or crazy but connected as they figure out their lives, too.

My hope is that this memoir will empower young women to embrace the messier parts of their lives. It's okay for y'all to fail, sometimes a lot, on the journey of life. When we embrace things not being perfect in a world that's increasingly geared toward perfection, that's when we get the chance to grow. That's when God gives us a great big opportunity—to learn to live and love a little better than we ever knew how to live before.

CHAPTER 1
Say What You Feel

My first night on *The Bachelorette*, right after meeting all the guys who were there to be my suitors, I wondered whether one of them might turn out to be my husband—and I sat there thinking, *I don't think he's here. I don't think he's here at all!*

I knew it was important for the guys on the show to be hopeful—to know that I was taking this seriously, and that I *did* see a future with one of them. So when the cameras were rolling, I gave this speech saying the exact opposite of how I felt. I basically said I believed my husband was in the room.

I said the words that I thought everybody wanted to hear me say. And even though I wanted those words to be true, it just felt wrong.

Later on, after a lot of reflection and more than a little therapy, I started to wonder why I did that.

My whole life, I'd been told to "say it like you mean it." To stand confident. Not just onstage (or on television), but in everyday life. But what good is saying it like you mean it if you don't say what you truly feel? Why did I do that?

Why, as women, do so many of us do that?

✳

My first concern when they filmed me getting out of the limo to meet host Chris Harrison in front of the *Bachelor* mansion was to do so without showing everyone my hoo-ha! My dress had a big slit in it, and pivoting out in a graceful and ladylike way was a real challenge. Once I finally managed it, I walked over to Chris wearing this heavy, nude-colored sequin gown that I could never afford myself. And from the very first step the gown kept getting sloshed with water, making it even heavier, until its weight literally cut off the circulation in my shoulder. (A TV "secret": they hose off the sidewalks and pavement so it all glistens in the lights. I never knew that, but now I notice it in all sorts of shows and movies. Like, *Huh. Why is the ground wet? It must rain a lot more than anyone realizes in Los Angeles!*)

Anyway, they dried my gown with a hair dryer, and I took my place in my high heels, with the gown getting all wet again at the bottom. Then Chris walked away, and all of a sudden it was silent. I mean, you could hear a pin drop.

Oh, my gosh, I thought, *this is it*. I couldn't believe this was really happening. But also, what the heck was I doing?

One by one the limos started coming up the driveway, and I felt like my heart was in my butt! Like my heart dropped so hard. Of course it was exciting, but it was also so much fear. I felt grateful, like pinch-myself grateful, but at the same time I was thinking, *What the heck am I doing trying to find a husband on TV?*

I was also super conscious of this massive zit on my face that showed up on that day. Of all days. Of course. I'd made it through all the preshow photo shoots and publicity with clear skin, and then right when I was gonna meet the guys, I got this massive cyst. I named it Marcus. And I swear I could feel Marcus growing bigger and bigger the whole night, as the guys got out of the limos, one by one, and came up to meet me for the very first time.

I worried that Marcus (and yes, we are still talking about the zit here) was all they'd see, not me! So the whole night I felt insecure. Which is kind of funny, since one of my primary goals that night was to make sure the *guys* didn't feel all awkward and insecure.

I remembered that awkward, nervous what-in-the-world-do-I-say feeling when I got out of the limo for the very first time to meet Colton, on the previous season of *The Bachelor*. The season where I went from being just one of the thirty girls he had to choose from to being heartbroken, talked about all over social media, and ultimately picked as the Bachelorette.

It's so quiet, I thought that first night on Colton's season. There were multiple crew people all standing there watching, and the lights were in my eyes, and I swear I started shaking like a fawn in head-lights in the middle of a four-lane freeway. I wished I had somebody there to guide me and let me know I'd be all right.

So when these guys got out, I just wanted to say, "It's okay! It's all gonna be okay. I felt the same way!"

As I stood there meeting the men one by one, other than my feet feeling like they were gonna fall off and the zit growing on my face, I enjoyed stepping into the experienced caregiver role for the guys, being the one to say, "I got this." I truly wanted to put the guys at ease. I cared more about them than I did about myself.

With most of the guys, I could see that their hands were shaky, that they couldn't put words together. But with the cameras rolling, I couldn't tell them, "Forget about the lights and all those crew people.

Just look into my eyes, and it's all gonna be okay." That would break the TV magic. So instead I just put on my perky pageant-girl smile and said, "Hi! I'm Hannah. So nice to meet you."

That's what I'm good at. When that internal pressure hits, I know how to turn it on. But these guys didn't know the Perfect Pageant Patty version of me. They had only ever seen me let loose on Colton's season. So when the time came for me to be the center of the show, the lead, the girl in charge of the situation, I did what needed to get done. I said what needed to get said. I smiled when I needed to smile. I poured my heart out when the situation required it.

But my true feelings? The real me? Where was she?

The answer's kind of murky.

I had always believed that when you meet somebody you're gonna have a spark with, you just know. And I didn't really get that feeling from any of the guys who got out of those limos.

Okay, I kept thinking. *Nice guy. Next one.*

Before the show started, before I gave up using my phone for those weeks, I had seen pictures of some of the potential suitors when they were leaked online by certain members of Bachelor Nation. (If you don't know, Bachelor Nation is what we call the rabid fan base in the social-media universe that follows every in and out of the show's existence, going back to the series' beginnings more than fifteen years ago.)

One of the guys I was kind of intrigued by was Tyler. He was really good-looking, and I wanted to find out what he was all about, but I kept waiting for him and waiting for him, to the point where I was standing there with my feet aching and my gown wet in the freezing cold—'cause it gets cold at night where the Bachelor mansion is located, high in Agoura Hills—thinking he must've been cut. But he finally showed up sometime after midnight. And the first thing I thought was, *Whoa! I think he's been drinking!*

It turns out he hadn't. He was just full of nervous energy. And when I finally got to gaze into his eyes, I felt a little connection. I felt a little spark. I felt a little connection with Jed, and with Luke, too, who I had met before this season even started.

But when the guys were all inside, I stepped through a side door into an interview room far from any of the guys' sight. While I was sitting there with my feet in a bucket of warm water, in a robe, clutching my Sulley pillow (you know, the cartoon character from the movies *Monsters, Inc.* and *Monsters University*) as someone blow-dried my gown again, that's when I thought, *I don't think he's here.*

I had heard about a previous Bachelorette who was disappointed on her first night because she didn't like any of the guys, and now she was married to one of them. But I didn't know that girl. I didn't know much of anything about what I had gotten myself into. I had never watched the show before joining Colton's season.

"Everybody kind of feels this way at first," I was reassured.

Wanting to be the good girl, wanting to prove that I could be the best Bachelorette ever, wanting to do anything I could not to disappoint anybody, I convinced myself to believe that somehow, this would all work out—and if I had a little faith, then maybe one of these guys would turn out to be the one after all.

"Okay," I said with a great big smile. And as a makeup artist made one final attempt to cover Marcus, I tipped my head back and asked, "Is there a booger in my nose?"

As I stepped back into in my blow-dried dress and those achy high heels, moments before walking to a room to see all thirty of those guys who had come to meet me, I knew I would need to make a speech. I'd started to work on the speech that day, and I had a pretty good idea that the guys—and all of Bachelor Nation—would expect me to say certain things. So I got ready to say all of those things in my speech, while trying to figure out how say them in my own words. I'd made plenty of speeches during my beauty-pageant career, which had ended only a year before this all started. I could be charming. I could be engaging. I wasn't afraid of public speaking at all. Pageants had given me that important life skill. But the idea that I might want to say something hopeful about seeing my husband in that room? It just wasn't sitting right with me.

So I changed it.

After thanking the guys for stepping away from their lives to have this uncharted adventure with me, I told them that I had come on *The Bachelor* to find my forever love—but what I'd actually found was myself. "I'm human, and so are you," I said. "I'm not looking for perfect. I'm looking for real. True love isn't perfect. It's beautiful, but it's also messy."

I looked around the room, making eye contact, trying desperately to make a real connection with someone, *anyone*. And I said, "In the few moments we've had together, you guys have made me feel like I deserve this. And for that I'm grateful for each and every one of you. I'm blown away . . . and I can see my husband being in this room."

Instead of saying "My husband is in this room," like I thought I was *supposed* to say, and instead of being honest and saying, "I just don't think any of you guys are it for me!" I found a safe middle ground: "I can see my husband *being* in this room."

(*Safe.* That's a word that comes up a lot with me.)

"Now raise your glass to find true, imperfect love!" I said. And we all raised our glasses of champagne.

Did I *wish* that my husband was in that room? Sure! Did I want true love? Absolutely! I'd grown up hearing all the crazy twists and turns various people took on the road to finding love, including the wild stories of what some people in the Bible went through on their journeys of faith, and I wanted to believe that there was no way God would put me through everything I'd been through—and put me on this show—if it wasn't going to lead to meeting the man of my dreams.

There's got to be a reason I'm here, I kept thinking. *Hannah, trust!*

But how much of that was me just rationalizing what I knew was wrong, in order to make it seem right? How much of that was me just playing a part in order to please everybody else? I became the person I needed to be, the person that everyone wanted me to be. Over the course of the season I played the part so well that in the end I even *believed* that it was me.

To be clear, I wasn't lying or faking it for anybody else. It was fun to meet all these guys. One of my favorite things to do is talk to strangers. I love meeting new people and finding connections—not necessarily in a physical or romantic way, but in a human way. So a part of me really enjoyed talking to these thirty strange men.

The pageant-girl side of me loved getting dressed up, looking pretty, *feeling* pretty, and putting on a good show, too.

And I loved that I was in charge. I had the power to send any of these guys home whenever I decided I'd had enough. Unlike with Colton, where he held the power, on *The Bachelorette* I held the power! But did I really have the power, when I didn't actually say how I was feeling?

Of course, having "power" isn't the ideal way to start a relationship. Any relationship. It's just not healthy. A relationship should be equal. But I didn't think about that then. There were too many other things to think about. Out of almost nowhere, I suddenly had my own television show. Chris Harrison was the host, but I was the lead, the drama, the fairy-tale princess, the protagonist. It was my responsibility not only to make this show but to find love while I did it.

That was a lot of responsibility! And because I didn't want to let anyone down, I didn't always express my true thoughts and feelings. Frankly, with all that pressure on me, there were times when I didn't even know what my true thoughts and feelings were.

So why am I bothering to tell *you* all of this?

Because I think life is that way, too. The company you work for, your teachers, your parents, your peer group, the influencers you see on TV and on social media—all of those people have a way of influencing what you think and what you do. And most of the time you don't even notice that it's happening, or what's getting lost along the way. I sure didn't.

Once you open your eyes to it, though, you start to notice it everywhere. Just like all that wet pavement on TV shows and in movies.

Once you see it, you start to question everything.

Mostly, you start to question yourself, and whether the decisions you've made in your life have truly been yours.

When I think back now to my first seasons in the world of reality TV, I get a knot in my stomach. This tightness in my chest. I can't even *remember* what was real and what wasn't. What was *me*, and what wasn't.

It wasn't the first time I had felt those feelings, and let me tell you, it's a scary place to be.

Do I regret going on *The Bachelor* or *The Bachelorette*? No! I learned so much through being on those shows—but what I learned wasn't about finding a husband. It was more about finding myself—and, at the same time, losing myself—just like I'd said in my speech. I would come full circle to learn that again in the days, weeks, and now years that followed.

As the world would soon find out, my engagement at the end of my season of *The Bachelorette* wouldn't last. It fell apart in the most soul-crushing way—because the man I chose had lied to me. He had lied to everyone. He had hidden his true circumstances from me, and from all of Bachelor Nation, too. His actions and choices were his own, but I also can't help but wonder if I had trusted my instincts at the start, or if I had spoken my true feelings out loud at a hundred different steps along the way—maybe if I had listened to myself instead of putting everyone else's feelings first—I wouldn't have gotten my heart broken so publicly, so humiliatingly, as I did.

What I'd learn over the course of the next year and a half is that all the hiding I did to make other people happy, all the twisting and turning, only hurt me in the end. And I didn't want to live like that anymore. I needed help. I needed friends. I needed therapy. God. I needed God therapy. I needed a lot, bless my heart!

What I really needed was to take some time to look back at my own life, to see where things went wrong and where they went right, and to rediscover and (hopefully) start to believe again in the person I really was.

CHAPTER 2
Put a Smile on Your Face

Identity is a funny thing. What we like, what we don't. Why we feel what we feel. The things that make us feel unique. The very things about ourselves that make us feel beautiful, or make us feel ugly. (I'm talking both inside and outside here.) The way we respond. The way we act. The strength we have. Our weaknesses. The confidence we show. The self-doubt we don't. All of it comes down to this crazy mix of what we're taught and what we're shown; what we grow up with and what we don't; what's buried deep in our DNA and what's right on the surface of what we witness every day.

Combine all that with the families we're born into, and the places we're raised, and the conditions of life in the towns or cities or countries we're raised in, and how in the heck are we supposed to sort through all of that and make sense of who we are?

People say things like, "Just be you, Hannah." Or, "Trust yourself." "Only you know how you really feel." "You'll have to make that decision on your own."

I can't tell you how many times I've heard phrases like these in my lifetime and thought, *Great. Thanks a lot. Did I miss a Hannah 101 class in school or something?*

All through life people say we should know ourselves, trust our guts, and listen to our hearts, as if there's some all-knowing self inside us that's completely ours alone. But how are we supposed to learn who that self really is?

I mean, honestly, would you be the same you if you were born somewhere else? If you looked different? If the people around you weren't the same people you always knew, and didn't influence you in the way they influenced you? How are we supposed to know who we are, when it's all such a jumbled-up mess from the start? When does the way you grew up stop, and who you really are begin?

I think the confusion for me started when I was a little girl in Alabama, over the littlest thing: my dimples.

Yes, dimples.

You wouldn't think somebody's dimples would cause some kind of existential *Who am I?* crisis, but that's kinda what they did for me. I had this big round face with round cheeks with these big squishy indents in them, which people always noticed. "Oh, look at those dimples!" they'd say while simultaneously pinching my cheeks without asking permission. The attention forced me to retreat behind my mom's legs and cling to her, just hiding and wishing and praying that everyone would stop noticing me and pointing out how I looked, because that meant, it seemed to me, that something about me was *weird*.

My friends didn't have big squishy indents on their faces. My Barbie dolls didn't have dimples, either. Neither did my American Girl dolls.

My dimples made me different, and I did not see that as a good thing.

Couple that with the fact that I used to smile all the time, and you can imagine how awkward and uncomfortable I felt as a little kid. Only nobody *knew* I was uncomfortable, because I smiled all the time and tried to hide whatever I was feeling. I learned really quickly that if you cried and fussed, adults paid attention. "What's wrong?" they'd say. "Is she okay?" I didn't want that kind of attention. So instead of fussing and crying, I smiled. And my smile only made my dimples more noticeable. Ugh!

Still, putting a smile on my face was always better than the alternative, which to me was the horrifying thought of making other people uncomfortable. I never wanted to do that.

"You're always smiling!" the adults would say. As if that was the best thing ever. As if smiling is what I was supposed to do. So I did—no matter what I was really feeling. The message I got before I was even in kindergarten was: you're not supposed to show emotion that isn't happy. So I turned every emotion into a smile.

Nervous? Smile. Happy? Smile. Worried? Smile. Hurt? Smile. People never knew that I had these really dark feelings because I always looked so happy. The smile was on the outside, but not always on the inside.

Of course, other kids (being honest in the way kids are) noticed, and sort of made fun of me for it. They would look at me smiling for no apparent reason and tease me. "What are you smiling at?" they'd say.

What I didn't realize until very recently is that my smile was a shield of sorts, a hedge of protection. If I smiled, no one questioned anything. So why would I ever lower that shield? Not just as a kid, but as an adult, too.

I've realized in these past couple of years that I've been using that shield my whole life. No matter what it was, I'd smile through it. I'd laugh through it. That's still the first instinct I go back to.

The smile is what I know and what I do to make sure nobody else is uncomfortable. Which of course begs the question: Why don't I care about my own comfort? If people are uncomfortable, isn't that their issue?

My mom didn't seem to notice the smile-to-hide-my-emotions part of me in my early years, and neither did I. In a way, I think we both saw my smile as a gift. After all, a smile brings warmth and comfort to others.

But thankfully my mom *did* notice how much I hated my dimples, and one day she decided to do something about it. Right around the start of second grade, she sat me down to watch some old Shirley Temple movies. They were full of singing and dancing, and so much fun and joy. They were great. Then she told me all about how Shirley Temple became a big famous Hollywood star—specifically *because* of her dimples.

Well, I thought. *That changes everything!*

I didn't realize people were pointing out my dimples because they *liked* them. I thought they were laughing at me. I thought they were pointing them out because I was some kind of freak for having these squishy holes in my cheeks that nobody else seemed to have.

Once I realized I could be proud of my dimples like Shirley Temple was, that made my smiling-shield habit that much easier to use.

Looking back, it's amazing to me how just one afternoon of watching Shirley Temple movies, getting just one little bit of new perspective on something I hated so much, could turn that something into a positive for me. It shifted the way I looked at myself and felt about myself and carried myself from that point forward.

My dimples were a part of what made me *me*. They were cool! They made me stand out—not like some kind of freak, but because there was something special about the way I looked.

I liked that.

The fact that a negative can so easily be turned into a positive with a little perspective shift is something I should have clung to and kept reminding myself of from that moment forward. How great would it have been if, all through my childhood and teen years and early twenties, I'd reminded myself that anything that felt bad or hurt me or made me feel "less than" could be changed if I just took a little time to look into it and change it? Change my perspective, change my attitude. Of course I didn't do that. Do any of us learn life lessons the first time we experience them? If so, I sure wish I could be that person! (Though I feel like that person is probably lying.)

For me it seems like I have to learn things again and again and again. Sometimes—as with this particular lesson—it can take me twenty years to finally get it. Which makes me wonder: What lessons am I learning right now that won't make sense to me till I'm forty-six? And what other lessons from my childhood do I still need to learn something from?

I was born in Tuscaloosa, Alabama, in September 1994, but I was raised in the town of Northport. I usually don't bother telling anybody that last part, unless they're from Tuscaloosa and know where Northport is. Northport is a small suburb. Not one-stoplight small, but a pretty typical *Friday Night Lights* kind of town, where football is everything and taking pride in your southern roots is just a given.

I didn't grow up in a neighborhood setting like most of my friends and schoolmates, though. Even though the city limit of Tuscaloosa was literally just across the street from my parents' house, we lived on seven acres, down a long driveway on a hilly property that could seem like it was in the middle of nowhere sometimes, in the shadow of a big ol' water tower. It was the kind of place where me and my friends and cousins could go outside and play Survivor all day, walking into the woods with a backpack full of Band-Aids and gummies, and pretend we were out in the wild. We'd sing Destiny's Child's "I'm a Survivor" while we picked up walking sticks we found on the ground and purposefully tried to get lost.

We tried to build bridges over the creek, and pretended we were being chased by monsters, like the make-believe Wampus cats my dad told me were out there hiding between the trees. (I think I believed Wampus cats were a real thing until I was fourteen years old.)

We were always scraping our knees and falling off our bikes, too, as we tried to ride them down the bumpy hills, all "Look! No hands!" That makes me sound like I was a tomboy, but I was just playing outside like everybody else did. I was fearless when I was young.

Unfortunately, Grace was not my middle name, and most of my fearless adventures ended up with fractured bones. I think I'd broken my wrists five times by the time I was in middle school. I swear I got hurt doing everything. I fell off a trampoline and broke my arm and my foot. I attempted to do this trapeze thing when I was in first grade, trying to imitate the acrobats I'd seen at the circus, only to come off the swing at its highest point, falling facedown on the concrete slab at the base. I hit so hard, I left a big chunk of chin on the concrete. There was so much blood, my mom passed out when she saw me. I guess I didn't "stick the landing" like I had anticipated. I broke both wrists when I hit the ground, and thank goodness for that, or I might've broken my neck. As it was, I suffered a concussion and got eighteen stitches in my face from that fall. You can still see the scar if you look really hard at some pictures of me, even though my mother had the surgeon try to fix me up right. I'm probably the youngest person to ever get a face-lift, as we always joke.

I broke my arm again at the Superskate on my birthday not long after that. Another time, I tried to get up to the top of a really tall slide by climbing up the support poles underneath it instead of using the ladder, and I fell off and broke my tailbone (though we wouldn't know that until later). My mom told me to brush it off and made me go to softball practice right afterward. She didn't take me to the hospital until I wouldn't stop crying about it all night.

I'm not sure why I was so fearless when I was little. But every time I got injured, it brought me attention. The first attention, with two broken wrists and a Band-Aid across half my face, I didn't want. But after that? I kind of liked that I got doted on, and it was cool to get friends to sign my casts—until the casts started to stink. That was *not* cool. But the fear of getting hurt made me less and less inclined to take those risks, because every time I took a risk, on a trampoline or even just skipping down the sidewalk sometimes, I ended up in a whole lot of pain. It was a lot for a little body to handle. (The trauma of those injuries has been long-lasting, by the way. I see a masseuse and a physical therapist today, and both of them have said that working on my body is more like working on a race-car driver than a former beauty queen!)

I suppose I could have spun it around like I did with my dimples, and looked at my scars as positive things: "Good experience." "Toughening me up." "Teaching me lessons about how to climb and jump and swing and bounce on the trampoline better the next time." But I didn't. I just slowed my enthusiasm down and started focusing on less dangerous activities. Part of that was easy to do, since my mother wasn't a fan of my pursuing sports. Playing in the yard?

Fine. She was happy I did that. But she wasn't a fan of softball, even though I loved it, because, she said, it was too "butch." (Her word, not mine!) So instead I did the thing she encouraged me to do: dance. She put me in dance classes starting when I was four years old, and I loved it—at first, at least. I loved the little outfits, and standing in front of the mirror, and learning new steps and routines. And it made my mom so happy to see me in the recitals.

The thing is, even while I was still in my tomboy stage, I was also the girliest girl imaginable. And isn't that okay? The only reason these two sides of myself seemed contradictory is that as a society we start slowly sending messages out that you have to choose who you are going to be—the class clown, the athlete, the southern belle, the nerd—and when you are forced to make that choice, you lose parts of who you really are. That's a message I wish I'd heard more as a little girl—that we can be more than one thing. It was totally okay for me to be playing Survivor *and* having my mom dress me in sparkly costumes and put bows in my hair!

Just to be clear: My mom didn't *make* me wear those girlie outfits. I *wanted* to look like the perfect little girl, from the perfect family, with the perfect smile. In fact, I wanted more than that. I wanted to *be* the good girl, too. I worked hard in school, and was the teacher's pet. I always sat up straight and paid attention in church. As I got a little older, I even carried a notebook into church so I could take notes on the sermons.

I believed it was okay for those two sides of myself to exist simultaneously. But sometimes society's old ideas of what a little girl should be are so strong that our truest selves are only expressed in what we imagine in our make-believe fantasy lives.

For example, my mom would buy me Barbies, and later American Girl dolls. She wasn't one of those moms who would get down on the floor and play dolls with me, though. I was left to play on my own. Which means I was left to my own imagination—and I think that was a really good thing.

Looking back, it strikes me that I never bothered to include a man in my imaginary doll worlds. Other girls I knew wanted to set up a wedding between Barbie and Ken every time they played. I didn't.

I rarely liked playing dolls with my friends because they didn't follow the storyline in my head. There was always a storyline, almost like a play, with a beginning, middle, and end. My mom worked from home during that time, and soap operas would be on during the day. The TV was always on. And that's how I did my dolls and Barbies. There was always a continuing storyline—only I can't recall ever including a man in any of those elaborate stories.

With my American Girl dolls later on, I was always playing the role of Mom—a single mom, mind you—and homeschool teacher. I took it so seriously, it was like method acting or something. I would get on the Internet to find printable worksheets, and give each doll a separate school folder. I drew up whole lesson plans. In my story I had adopted all these kids from around the world. I didn't have a husband, and there were no romantic relationships in any of this. I just didn't think about it at the time. My Barbies didn't have boyfriends. None of them. I had bride Barbies dressed in beautiful wedding dresses, but they weren't getting married to a *man*. They would just have the celebration.

How crazy is it that I grew up to become a girl known for looking for love—and marriage—on TV?

I know this sounds weird, but whenever I found out that my much-older sister or my babysitters had a boyfriend, it made me sad. I didn't understand why they *needed* a boyfriend.

My mom and dad showed affection to each other sometimes. So

it wasn't that I didn't see any love in our house or anything like that. I just didn't think about having a boyfriend, or my dolls having a boyfriend, because I did not care. And when I *did* think about it, I was like, "That is waaaaaay in the future." Most of the time, if anybody asked me about it, I would tell them I was planning to marry myself. That sounded like way more fun, and a lot less of a hassle.

In my earliest years I didn't see the supposedly very southern ideal of marrying a man as some sort of ultimate achievement. It didn't seem like a fairy tale come true to me. Even as I got older, say third or fourth grade, I remained a fiercely independent thinker.

I think I got some of my spirited, independent girl-power sentiment from watching Ellen and Oprah after school every day. There was something about the way those women would talk to people and get them to open up about their lives that I just loved, whether it was Ellen's way of being funny, joking around with her guests and dancing with her audience—just for fun, just because it feels good—or Oprah's ability to cut right to the heart of the matter and bring tears to everyone's eyes. These women were in *charge*. They were *stars*. They didn't need a man beside 'em to run those shows. They were the bosses themselves, and I loved that.

I didn't just like *watching* them. A part of me dreamed about *being* a talk show host. Even back then, I loved talking to people, including perfect strangers. I liked learning about other people's lives, especially when they were excited to tell me about something they were really good at or passionate about.

There were days when me and my best friend, Olivia, would go into the bathroom and play talk show all afternoon. Olivia and I were like twins in some ways. We were born three months apart, our moms were best friends, and we spent so much time together that we spoke our own language when we were little. So imagining we were going to be talk show hosts together was easy, and we used the bathroom because it was the only room in the house with anything close to a curtain on a stage. We'd work it all out and then perform for each other, taking turns sitting on the toilet seat as the studio audience. We would practice all day, and when her mom came to pick her up we'd announce ourselves and pull the shower curtain back and then stand up on the edge of the tub, cracking jokes and doing interviews like we were on TV.

Given my attraction to being the host, the boss, the single mom and homeschooler with a classroom full of adopted kids, I guess you could say I was an independent thinker at a young age. But I would rarely express those independent thoughts of mine anywhere outside our home, because, like I said, outside our home I wanted to be perfect. And being perfect meant fitting into a certain box that a good Christian southern girl was supposed to stay in.

There was this one time, though, I think in second grade, when my lack of dreaming about attention from boys caught up with me. This boy who really liked me approached me outside school on Valentine's Day, on the sidewalk, at the drop-off line where everyone's moms dropped us off for the day. Right where everyone could see. And he handed me a stuffed teddy bear and said "Happy Valentine's Day!" and I just about died. I was so embarrassed!

It felt like everybody stopped and looked right at us, like the whole world stopped moving and the cars all came to a screeching halt. And without even thinking, I threw that teddy bear on the ground and said, "No!" I ran inside as fast as I could to hide in the classroom and get on with my day, hoping and praying that everyone would forget about what just happened. Especially him.

The classroom was usually a comforting place for me—mainly because I could be the "good girl" there. I could get the As. I could make the best projects, all on my own. (Although my parents were very involved in my schooling, they were sticklers about me doing all my work myself. That allowed me to feel really good when I got an A, knowing that nobody else did the work for me.) My teachers always loved me because I smiled all the time and tried to be helpful. And I felt confident I could win whatever contests came up, too. I was sure of it. Because if I thought I *couldn't* win, I would do my best to avoid competing in the first place.

Winning mattered to me because it felt *good*, on both the inside and the outside.

But not winning? Messing up? Looking bad in front of other kids and adults? That hurt me.

For some reason, that hurt me really bad.

CHAPTER 3

STAY INSIDE THE LINES

I mentioned that my parents wanted me to do my school projects myself, and wouldn't do the work for me or even help me much the way some other parents clearly did with their kids. But what they *would* do is buy me pretty much anything I wanted or needed to get those projects done—including all the brand-new crayons I could get my hands on. I don't know what this says about me, but I *loved* crayons. Not just any crayons, but specifically the Crayola crayons that came in the big box of sixty-four. I loved all the colors, and their waxy smell and just-right shape. They had to have the tips, though. I couldn't stand it when they got worn down. The idea of sharpening them? Trying to use them when they weren't perfect, like when they turned into a little nub with the paper torn off? Ew. No. They just weren't the same as those brand-new, right-out-of-the-box crayons.

So my parents would buy me a new box of sixty-four Crayola crayons probably every two weeks—until we found the giant boxes of a hundred and twenty Crayola crayons at Walmart one day. That made me really excited, just dreaming about putting all of those colors into my coloring books and artwork. They started buying me new sets every couple of weeks as part of my mom's regular shopping trips.

I can't even tell you how proud it made me to always have the best crayons at Huntington Place Elementary School.

My dad, the hairstylist, the creative one in the family, sat me down one night when I was very young and taught me how to color in a way I never forgot. "Make a hard, dark line of the color just perfectly inside the line," he told me, "almost like a template to make sure that you don't go outside the line—because you *cannot* go outside the line."

I took that to heart.

I went above and beyond to get it just right when coloring the inside of any picture, too. I'd color the pictures in until there was no white space left at all. *None.* That's not easy to do with crayons, but that's what I did, because I thought that's what looked right. It took a lot more effort, but it was so much more precise. And perfect. And *beautiful.*

For some reason, my entire life, I have been drawn to beautiful things. Beautiful paintings, beautiful homes, beautiful scenery, beautiful fabrics and clothes, curtains and bedding—it doesn't matter what it is. If it's beautiful, I'm drawn to it. And learning to color gave me the ability to create something beautiful all by myself, which I just thought was the greatest thing ever.

When my first-grade teacher started holding coloring contests for every holiday, I entered those contests. And I *won.* I did the best coloring of a Thanksgiving turkey, and then I did the best Christmas coloring, and Valentine's coloring. I won a lot of coloring contests!

I loved that feeling. I loved the attention I got for winning. I also felt tremendous pride: the pride of working hard and getting recognized for putting the effort in to make something beautiful. It was so different from the kind of attention that made me uncomfortable, because it was the first time, really, that it was for something I was *doing*. And I wanted to keep winning.

I wanted to move beyond just coloring in other people's drawings, and learn how to draw myself. So I got my mom to buy me some teach-yourself-how-to-draw books, and I learned how to draw a dog, real easy, starting with six circles. Then a ballerina, with a tutu and a ballet bun. I started doodling in the pages of my notebooks and drawing every chance I got.

Then Easter came around, and my teacher decided to change things up. Instead of a coloring contest on paper, she decided to hold an Easter-egg-coloring contest in the classroom, using watercolor paints—something I'd never been shown how to use.

I was excited to jump right into it. We'd been taught all about the primary colors and how they blend—like mixing blue and yellow gives you green, and mixing red and blue gives you purple. I was convinced that I could make the prettiest egg of them all by mixing the colors just like we'd been taught. Plus, I had dyed eggs at home, and I'd watched my mom create tie-dye looks, mixing different colors by dipping the egg directly into the dyes to blend colors. I came up with a whole design idea in my head that would have all sorts of pretty colors from top to bottom, and I mixed my dyes and paints and got to work—and my egg turned this pukey greenish-brown color.

I had no idea that that's what happens when you try to mix watercolors together.

I was shocked. I looked over at everyone else's really simple, pretty, basic pastel eggs, and could not believe how ugly mine looked. But before I could even ask my teacher what I'd done wrong and learn how to color an egg with watercolors without turning it brown, two of my very best friends saw what I'd done and started making fun of me. They were so loud about it that suddenly everyone was laughing at my puke-colored egg. I was so embarrassed, and so sad.

My egg didn't turn out the way I wanted it to on the first try, and I might have been okay with it if I'd been given a minute to learn what I'd done wrong and maybe try it again. But when those girls started to make fun of it and didn't stop, I was upset. It got so bad that my teacher had to step in to get them to stop laughing and acting so mean and try to calm me down. It crushed me.

Honestly, I think I could have accepted that my egg looked rotten if my friends hadn't judged me and made such a big deal about it in front of everybody in that classroom. But once that happened, I was done.

I don't mean I was just done for the day, or done painting Easter eggs in school. I mean that after that happened, I didn't want to be creative anymore. I pretty much stopped coloring and drawing from that day forward. I didn't even doodle in my notebooks. I would still do coloring books sometimes, mostly at home, because I thought I was still good at that. But as far as being creative in any sort of a public way, in competitions, in front of my peers? I just stopped.

I wanted this egg to be really special, and creative, and *different* from the average egg—and I failed. And the lesson I took away from that wasn't "Try again, you'll do better next time." The lesson was "Don't go outside the lines, Hannah. You're good at staying in the lines. Stay there."

Looking back, it was a lot like all of those times I'd taken some big, crazy risk on the playground and landed flat on my face. The lesson I learned was the same: Stop taking risks. Stay inside the lines. I took that criticism to heart in a big way, thinking, *Okay, other people* do *know better than me.*

I was too young to understand the deeper psychological impact of that moment, of course, but I for sure took it to heart. From that point forward, I would stay inside the lines, stay in the box, more and more every year. Especially whenever any kind of potential for public humiliation existed. I'd learned my lesson: in the box, I did well, but when I stepped out of the box, I didn't.

I think of the drawings that never happened. The coloring books I never filled. Because of that one incident, I never learned how to paint.

I never related my decision-making process at that time to the egg incident, but now that I look back on it, it seems crystal clear.

For example, I thought volleyball looked really fun, but I never even tried it. I convinced myself that I couldn't take it up because I didn't know if I was any good at it. I stuck with dance because I was good at dance. Not the best, but good enough. It made my mom happy. I knew what I was doing in dance. But volleyball? I was scared to even try because I didn't want to be *bad* at something. I wanted to look good and *be* good—for my parents, for my teachers, and in front of my friends.

That same way of thinking would keep me from trying new things, again and again, in all sorts of subtle ways. I became more timid. I made myself stay in my lane. In my box. Inside the lines.

Why was it so important to me that others didn't see me make mistakes? Why did my desire to be seen as the perfect little good girl outside my home matter so much back then that I would let one incident shut me down?

Why does it *still* matter so much to me?

The thing I've come to realize is that maybe, just maybe, it has something to do with the fact that my home life wasn't the kind of "perfect" I wanted and needed it to be.

CHAPTER 4
Sweet Home Alabama

The one place I was always happy, no matter what else was happening in my life, was in the sunshine. At the beach, especially. We didn't go very often as a family because it was a four-hour drive to get to the shore. My parents said it got too hard to take me when I was a baby, because every time we went I would wind up with some kind of diaper rash or bladder infection from the sand, or the water, or something. So they stopped going to the beach, and instead they built us a pool in our backyard.

It was beautiful. It felt like we had our own personal country club right outside our back door—which is pretty amazing, considering that both of my parents grew up poor.

My mom grew up in a real small town. I'm talking a no-stoplight town, on a mountain, where everybody knew everybody, in a community where the church was basically her extended family. Only the church she went to wasn't the Loving God–type church that so many of us think of today when we think of a place of worship. Her church was a Southern Methodist church with sermons full of fire and brimstone, where she was taught to be "God fearing," as if she should feel guilt and shame for every little bad thought she had or misdeed she'd ever done. But my mom was a hellion. She was like one of the rebellious kids in the movie *Footloose*, just cutting loose and trying to have fun no matter what the adults said.

She was just eighteen years old when she first met and fell in love with my dad.

Eighteen. She was just a kid.

When she had me, nearly eight years later, it was almost like she got to live her childhood all over again—without the fire and brimstone, and without some other big struggles she had that I'll talk about a little bit later. Only this time, she got to live it through *me*.

Did you ever see the movie *Hope Floats*? It's a good one if you haven't. Sandra Bullock stars as a married woman who goes on a TV show thinking she's getting a makeover, only to get told on TV that her husband was cheating on her. With her whole world shattered, she goes back home to Texas, where to everyone else it looked like she was always Little Miss Perfect. Back in her hometown she was not only the homecoming queen, she was Miss Cream of Corn! "There was a time when your momma shined, too," she says to her daughter.

When Sandra's character gets home after the TV fiasco, though, her own momma says to her, "Have you took up drinking? You look horrible!"

The gist of *Hope Floats* is that when Sandra Bullock's character was growing up, she found her mom to be more than a little embarrassing, and she felt it was her responsibility to be Miss Everything in order to make up for the way her mom was.

That's how I felt sometimes, too. Almost exactly.

My mom wasn't a taxidermist like the fictional character in the movie, though. My mom was the mama with big boobs who would tell somebody off to their face if she thought they deserved it. She wasn't just blunt and up-front with me. She was blunt and up-front with *everybody*. Oh, and the boobs I'm referring to? She got a boob job after she gave birth to me and my little brother. She didn't want to look like one of those tired old moms with saggy boobs, she said. So she went out and did something about it. And she was proud to let anyone who asked, or who stared at her in her tight and sometimes embarrassingly revealing tops, know it.

She was, without a doubt, the "hot mom."

I was pretty young when I remember asking her why she dressed so differently than the other moms did, in their conservative matching sweater sets. She must've been barely in her thirties then, and she looked at me and said straight up, "I'm not gonna dress like an old woman, Hannah."

The thing about *Hope Floats* is that even though there were some truly bad parts of the mom character, it's clear that all of her intentions were good and from the heart. You come away from that film still loving the mom. And I feel the same way about my mom. She would do anything for me.

But some moms—like the one in *Hope Floats*—love too hard, and my mom could be like that at times.

I think parents can love too hard in a lot of different ways, but my mom loved too hard by living vicariously through me as I danced through my childhood and on into the pageant universe. (In therapy these last few years, I've learned the term for that: codependency. It's as if she depended on me to fulfill her happiness, instead of finding happiness in herself. And I wanted to make her happy and proud, too!) Her attachment to and enthusiasm for everything I did felt smothering at times, yet still I bent over backward to please her. I was attached to her, too! Sometimes she had to tell me to go play outside because I kept clinging to her.

I bent over backward to please my dad, too, only the way he loved too hard was to always be scared that something was going to happen to us, like we were gonna mess up, or fail, or go broke, or hurt ourselves. His response to that fear was to always be telling us, "Don't do it." Honestly, there are too many times to count when I didn't do something I wanted to do because of that overly worried voice of his ringing in my ears. I think his being so worried all the time was a way of controlling my brother and me.

But can I blame my parents for being controlling? My mom was only twenty-six when she had me. That's about the same age I am now! The only thing I'm giving birth to at twenty-six is this book (okay, fine, I'm twenty-seven, but I was twenty-six when I wrote it), and that's stressful enough! I can't imagine how complicated my life would be if I tried to add a baby into the mix at this age. I truly can't. How would I cope with all of the things I'm going through while somehow putting the right kind of love and time and effort into raising a child, too? I'm not sure I'd be prepared to raise a child at this age. What would I be giving up? What would I gain? Just thinking about these things gives me so much more empathy for what it must've been like for my mom trying to raise me back then.

Most of my friends from back home are already married, and most have had a baby, if not two. God bless them, because I don't think I would be capable of getting through it. It may be the norm in Alabama, but maybe I've always been on a different path.

My dad had a child even younger than my mom did, with another woman, before he met my mom. (My dad's nine years older than my mom.) My older half sister, Alisa, is thirteen years older than me. She was a full-blown teenager by the time I had my first memories of her, and she moved out when I was still a little girl. But she played a big role in my mom and dad getting together in the first place.

My dad was a hairstylist in town, and my mom didn't take a shine to him immediately. (A lot of other girls did, from the stories I've heard. Being a straight hairstylist is apparently a really great way to meet women.) But this one time, they ran into each other at Wendy's. My dad had taken Alisa there for lunch, and my mom was there getting a hamburger while recovering from a hangover after a night out with her friends. They sat together, and my mom and Alisa got along real good. Alisa couldn't stop talking about her afterward. She kept saying my mom looked "just like a Barbie doll," with her blond hair and blue eyes—and then my dad couldn't stop thinking about her either.

They started spending more and more time together, and they fell in love. At first my mom wasn't sure she wanted to be with a guy who was so much older than she was, and who already had a daughter. But her dad, my grandfather, told her, "You don't get to pick who you fall in love with." So my mom just followed her heart and jumped into the marriage.

My mom used to repeat that phrase to me all the time, so it's ironic that I ended up going on a reality TV show with the express goal of picking who I'd fall in love with. But the way she explained that phrase was more of a warning for my heart. Like, "Be careful who you let your heart open to, because you don't get to pick who you fall in love with sometimes. And you have to be ready for whatever comes with that, once you've made the decision to put your heart out there."

I've definitely learned that the hard way these last couple of years.

I guess to some people there's something really unique and kinda cool and romantic about my parents' story, the way they didn't let a big difference of age or a child from a prior relationship stand in the way of their love for each other. But I said this on TV, and I know they heard it because I was sitting on the couch right next to them watching my season of *The Bachelorette* when I said it, so I think it's safe to say it here again: I don't *want* the kind of marriage my parents have. I appreciate that they love each other, and they've stuck it out and done everything they could to make it work, and I know they always worked as hard as they did to support my brother and me. But I could see—even from a very young age—that their relationship could be toxic at times.

The ugly truth is that their marriage consisted of a lot of built-up resentment, a lot of fighting, a lot of harsh words and threats of leaving that they yelled at each other in the middle of the night, using language that I would never, ever want to hear in my own marriage. It's bad enough that I had to hear it as a little girl, hiding in my bedroom.

In so many ways, after trying to rebel against her strict upbringing, my mom wound up playing the role of the good southern wife. And I'm so thankful for that! I knew I could count on my mom to be there, no matter what, and that was such a gift. This came after putting herself through college, and doing her best to be a strong, independent woman. She loved being a stay-at-home mom for us at first, to be the mom she never really had, to be present for us at school, as a volunteer, alongside the full-time unpaid position of taking care of the entire household. But I don't think there's any such thing as a stay-at-home mom. She was always on the go and doing more than that. The older we got, the more it seemed like she was always working for my dad directly, too, as a sort of partner in the business: doing the books and helping to manage the day-to-day tasks, but with no credit and nothing in particular to show for herself. She didn't earn a paycheck. She didn't have her own money, which meant she didn't have her own freedom. *And she knew it.*

My mom raised me to be smart and do well in school so I could be "independent," she said. So I wouldn't have to "depend on a man." And I heard those words when she said 'em. They stuck with me, obviously, or I wouldn't be repeating them here in this book. But what I saw at home was her working her tail off just trying to keep up the household and being entirely dependent on my dad, even when he yelled at her. She had no choice but to stay in that marriage, because where was she supposed to go? She didn't have a résumé to speak of. She didn't have a degree—not just because she married young, but because she quit school to care for her own mother when her mom tried to commit suicide. (I'll share more details about this in a later chapter.) So truly, she was stuck. And that dysfunction showed up in our home in all sorts of different ways.

We rarely ate meals together at the kitchen table. The table was covered in a pile of laundry and usually some paperwork, since it served as my mom's makeshift office. If we ate together at all, it was at the coffee table in front of the TV, or on whatever surface wasn't piled up with all kinds of other stuff. Our house wasn't dirty. It was just chaotic. It was never, ever anything close to the showplaces that so many of my friends' houses seemed to be.

We said grace over our food sometimes, but it wasn't a consistent thing at all. We didn't go to church with any consistency, either. We went more than just Easter and Christmas, but there was no rhyme or reason to it. If me or my brother woke up late on Sunday morning and said we didn't want to go, my parents pretty much shrugged their shoulders and said, "Okay."

Noooo! I thought. I desperately wanted them to make us go to church, and to make us say grace before every meal, and to ask me questions about scripture the way I saw and heard my friends' parents do.

I just couldn't understand why we lived so different than they all did. I wanted more structure. I wanted more God. I craved for everything to be a little less chaotic.

I mentioned already that my dad was a hairstylist, and that fact all by itself made us "different." All the other kids' dads were doctors, or lawyers, or construction workers. Some of them were professors at the University of Alabama. But nobody else's dad was a hairstylist. I got made fun of relentlessly for that. Kids would bully me and say my dad must be gay just because of his job. (Welcome to Alabama in the mid-2000s!) My seventh-grade teacher made fun of my dad and his profession one day, in front of the whole class. And it all got so confusing. There were times when I questioned whether my dad might actually be gay, just because he did something creative. That was before I really knew what *gay* meant. I thought it was just some sort of a bad word, because that's how kids used it. Once I knew better, I knew for sure my dad wasn't gay (not that there's anything wrong with that), but then I kept wondering, *Why would that be a bad thing anyway? And why did I deserve to be picked on and made fun of because of it?*

My dad provided for us. Over time he went from owning his own salon to opening a series of schools in the Paul Mitchell cosmetology franchise, where he taught all kinds of other people how to be hairdressers, too. This was a man who at one point was sleeping in his car while he tried to save enough money to find an apartment. He should have been hailed as one of those great, all-American success stories, since he started from nothing and pulled himself up by his bootstraps again and again. He kept a roof over our heads and food on the table—even though he'd complain and even yell at times about how much my mom spent on groceries every week. I'm not sure why he got so angry about money all the time, since his businesses did really well. People thought we were rich, though we weren't, and that caused them to look down on us in a way because we had some nice things but my father wasn't a doctor or a lawyer. And to be looked down on when he worked so hard made him mad. When he did come home, he was exhausted, and that made home life hard. Maybe it's because he'd been made fun of, too. Maybe it's because he'd been poor as a kid. I'm not sure. But he did well enough, especially with my mom's help, that my parents were able to buy me pretty much anything I ever wanted or needed.

It was weird, though. There was always tension around money. My mom would take me school shopping, and we'd come home from the mall with multiple bags full of clothes sometimes. But then when my dad came home and wanted to see what we bought, my mom would tell me to bring out only one bag. We had to hide all the rest so she wouldn't have to hear it from him!

There was good reason for that: when my dad got mad, it was awful.

My dad has changed a lot in recent years, and has mellowed out a lot overall, but back then, when he got mad it was almost like he turned into a different person. When he was fun and silly, he was the best! But then a switch got hit, and the anger was just so completely out of nowhere, and out of proportion compared to anything that had happened. Like, if we spent too much money in any given week he told us we were going to have to live in a refrigerator box.

My parents got into fights at night often, fights I'd hear from my bedroom. And sometimes they would carry on the next morning, while I was getting ready for school. I walked on eggshells. I didn't want to be the reason they fought. And I don't think there was any part of me that wanted to be in a marriage after witnessing that kind of anger and bickering.

✳

Throughout most of my childhood, my dad's focus was on work. When he got home, exhausted, it felt like he wouldn't really listen or seem to care about much of what we were up to. But then something would grab his attention and he would get mad that he didn't know what was going on, insisting that we "didn't tell him things." He would yell at Mom for that. And she would never just let him yell at her. She would argue back. Because that's what she always did. Even though she gave up a lot for him, she still had that feisty, rebellious mountain blood in her. The arguments would escalate. They would say the most horrible things to each other.

How can you say horrible things and *yell* horrible things at the person you love, and then come back from that? Again and again?

How is that even love?

When I was in high school, my dad left for two weeks and stayed at one of his businesses. On his way out the door that morning, just as I woke up for school, he yelled at my mom that he didn't love her anymore, that he was "done."

Two weeks later he came back, and everyone acted like nothing had ever happened.

But I didn't forget. I held the weight of their relationship, even as a kid, because my mom would share things with me about what the relationship was like, and what he would say to her. But what can a ten-year-old do? What can a fourteen-year-old do? I was treated more like her confidante than her child sometimes. I know now how unhealthy that really was, but I wanted nothing more than to make the fighting stop, to make her happy, to make *him* happy.

Is it any wonder that I did everything I could to be the peace-maker? I didn't want to be one more reason for the dysfunction in the family. I wanted to be the reason for everything to be okay. Which meant: How many 100s could I get on tests? How many As on my report card? On some days, being the star student was enough of a distraction to bring peace to the family.

My parents' relationship had a direct effect on my relationship with my brother, too. My brother, Patrick, was two and a half years younger than me, and I resented him so much. He was always doing something "wrong." He was a rambunctious kid, a toddler, he didn't know any better, but night after night he would stand in front of the TV. Like, right in front of it. And my dad would yell at him, and then it would become an argument between my parents, because my mom would just tell him to let Patrick be. She always had something to say.

The way I saw it back then was Patrick's misbehaving caused fights, which made me try even harder to do anything I could to *not* cause fights.

Once he was a little older, we found out that Patrick had trouble with his eyesight. That's why he was standing in front of the TV. He just wanted to see it! Later in high school, he was also diagnosed with ADHD. Looking back on it, none of us should have been so quick to judge his behavior. He was just a kid! But back then my dad insisted that his behavior was my mom's fault. And the fact that Patrick made them get into arguments made me want to take out all my anger on *him*. And I did. Not only did I tell him to go away all the time and try to keep him from playing with my friends, but we'd get into physical fights when he refused to move, or wouldn't listen to me. And sometimes I was really aggressive.

Whenever I was being mean to my brother, my mom would say,

"Hannah, you're being mean as a snake." And I'll admit there were times when I was. I still am sometimes! But I spent so much energy trying to be the perfect girl at school that I would come home exhausted. I just couldn't take any more, and Patrick acting up or causing trouble was the last straw.

Why was I so exhausted? Because I was performing all day. Trying to be perfect, because I felt like I had to. In fact, my mom would come home from parent-teacher conferences saying, "Your teachers all said you were so sweet. They have no idea that you're here at home beating up on your little brother."

Then she'd take me to dance class, where I'd get even more exhausted, doing everything I could to try to please her.

All I wanted was for my mom to feel happy. To feel loved. And I convinced myself that if I was good and perfect, then she would be happy.

I'm grateful for my parents for giving my brother and me so much. I'm even grateful that they stayed together, because things have gotten a lot better between them over these last few years. But it sure wasn't easy. I didn't have anyone to talk to about any of it. And I blamed myself a whole lot. I would pray to God, begging, even screaming sometimes, for their fighting to stop. Then when God didn't answer those prayers, I thought it was because I didn't always go to church, or because my family didn't go over my scriptures with me.

It was all just so confusing, and so hard to make sense of as a little girl.

*

Wishing I could be Oprah or Ellen, living out the single-mom storylines with my dolls, taking the constant lessons about "independence" I heard from my mom to heart, I had all the signs of turning into a budding young feminist as a kid. But *feminist* was like some sort of bad word in the South.

I remember going to church and learning from the Bible that a woman is supposed to be "submissive," but no one really explained what *submissive* means. The message I wrote in my notes at the time was that if you're "a good Christian woman," that means you're gentle, serving, and quiet. (Which y'all know isn't exactly how I turned out.)

Even the tried-and-true marriage vows made the point that a woman is supposed to "cherish, honor, and obey" her husband. No one ever talked about another interpretation of those vows: that it's important to respect your husband and "obey" your commitment to each other. I personally do *not* think it means that the woman is supposed to be ordered around by her man. But that kind of thing was hardly ever discussed in the South, and most people seemed to believe that "obeying" her husband's every word was the upright Christian thing for a woman to do. I wouldn't hear anything about the more human, more feminist, yet no less Christian interpretation of that vow until I was in college; that whole idea was just way too "liberal" for most southerners I encountered. And the southerners I knew were really good people! That's the thing. There wasn't any part of me that wanted to rebel against what I was seeing. I wanted to be the good girl for so many reasons at the time.

I didn't want to be a feminist, especially after I saw a picture of a bunch of feminists gathered to protest the Miss America pageant in 1968. I was doing research for a history project on the pageant, which I loved, when I found this photo of a bunch of angry-looking women holding their bras clutched in their fists up over their heads, and most of 'em hadn't shaved their armpits!

Given the perfect little good-girl image I was trying to make everyone see in me, and how much I dreamed about becoming Miss

America myself one day, that picture made me think that a feminist was the last thing I ever wanted to be.

Now, I don't want my childhood to seem all bad. It wasn't. Not at all. I think that's one thing that's so hard about looking back and trying to figure out why we are the way we are, and why we do the things we do: nothing in our histories is ever clearly black-and-white. It's just that the fights and trouble, the traumatic events, loom a little larger in our memories for some reason. (Just like negative comments tend to loom way larger than all the good comments when they show up in our social-media accounts, am I right?)

One of the real blessings I had is that I was always surrounded by wonderful older kids and young women. The girls who worked the front desks at my parents' businesses, the older children of my parents' friends, even my parents' friends themselves were all so loving and kind and supportive of everything I did. Being around girls who were going to college and making their own money and pursuing their own careers was inspiring to me. Some of them served as real mentors, others would take me shopping, and I just appreciated them so much. I looked up to them and wanted to learn from them, and I always knew I had a cheering section, which would help give me confidence in the future when I stepped into the pageant world and when I applied to college. Because of my parents, I had this amazing community in my life, outside of school. And that mattered.

I also had the best babysitter in the world. Casey Rae started out working at my parents' tanning salon and babysat Patrick and me only occasionally, but the busier my parents got, the more and more she started staying with us from 7:00 a.m. till 7:00 p.m.

Casey went to the University of Alabama, where she joined a

sorority and was a cheerleader, and she taught me all kinds of cheers and dances just for fun. I remember learning routines from *Bring It On* with her, and she put my hair up in a high ponytail. We watched *Dawson's Creek* together. But it was more than just the fun stuff I loved. Casey grew up in a very small home, her parents had split up, and then she lost her dad at a young age. Life wasn't easy on her, and yet she made the best of everything and kept moving forward. She was going to school to become a nurse, to take care of other people. I found that so inspiring, and I loved the way she took care of me. She would pick me up for school, and we would talk about my boy troubles (as I got a little older, I mean). She went on family trips with us, and took me and Patrick to the water park. It was like having a bonus older sister.

I had other older friends who went to different schools, too. I don't think I would have made it if I didn't have a community and friends. And when it came right down to it, no matter what was going on, my parents really did love me.

I've already said that my mom was the best mom. And there were times when I felt that way about my father, too. There were plenty of times when my brother, Patrick, and I got along just fine. A lot of times, my childhood in Alabama was really fun, and full of laughter.

Especially at our backyard pool.

I learned how to swim on my dad's back, and I swear we would swim every day all summer long. All my mom's friends and their kids came over to our house once that pool was built, and it was *so fun*. We'd eat watermelon and popsicles and play Marco Polo from 10:00 a.m. till it was dark outside—and then we'd go night swimming! We'd go skinny-dipping as little kids sometimes. And then we'd run out into the hills and catch fireflies or frogs.

Because of that childhood, I don't like to wear shoes outside, ever.

When I'm back home, my feet are always callused and built up from walking on the hard ground and dirt and rocks without a care in the world. Honestly, my heaven would be to spend my days walking on the greenest, plushest grass, on the edge of a beautiful ocean and a beach with sand that doesn't get stuck everywhere. Of all the things I did as a kid, playing in the pool, running around in the Alabama sunshine—that's when I smiled the most. That's when my smile was *real.*

I smiled that smile a lot.

Other times? At school, at dance, at home? Right up through these last couple of years? I'm painfully aware now that my smile, dimples and all, rarely stopped being my mask. A weapon. A shield. The veil I used to cover up the dysfunction of the family I grew up in—and the pain and shock of an unexpected trauma that none of us ever saw coming.

CHAPTER 5

The Man at the Door

I'll never forget the date: Friday, May 11, 2001. It was the day of my dance recital. I was six years old, and my mom had me hoisted up on the counter by the bathroom sink. My hair was in a high ponytail, with a full set of rollers weighing my head back. My mom was doing my makeup, so I could be stage-ready to perform my jazz routine in my sequined costume.

It was the biggest night of the year for me as a young dancer, performing for a crowd of proud family and friends. My dad came into the bathroom while I was getting ready.

"Are you excited to see me dance pretty?" I asked him.

"I'm sorry, honey. I have to go help your Aunt LeeLee. I'm not going to be able to make it."

My mom and dad exchanged a look that I didn't understand, and my dad turned and left the bathroom real quick. I heard him leave the house and take off in his car, and my little heart sank with disappointment.

Why would Daddy miss my special night?

My young intuition knew something was wrong, but my mom kept putting on my pretty pink blush and black mascara. I could tell in the look she exchanged with my dad that something was wrong, and I could see in her eyes that she was not okay. Something was making her upset. But she continued to encourage me and get me ready to take the big stage.

My recital went well, and I loved being onstage so much, but the disappointment of not seeing my daddy there really bothered me. So did the way my mom was smiling, as if she was trying to force it. She usually glowed after a recital, as if she'd been up there dancing herself.

Saturday came and went, and my father never came home. It felt . . . it all felt so strange.

Sunday was Mother's Day, and my dad was still gone.

"He's still in Hamilton," my mom said.

That's Hamilton, Alabama, where Aunt LeeLee lived with her husband, my Uncle Stu, and their two kids, our cousins Robin and Trent, in a beautiful house they'd just finished building. Robin and Trent were almost the exact same ages as me and my brother Patrick—six and four—and we were just about as close as cousins could be. They were not only our family but two of our very best friends, all wrapped into one. And my dad seemed closer to Aunt LeeLee than just about anyone else on his side of the family. Especially in those last few months, since their mom, my MawMaw, had passed away just that past December. Even so, no matter what it was that Aunt LeeLee needed help with that weekend, I just couldn't understand why Daddy wouldn't be home by now to celebrate Mother's Day with us.

I kept asking my mom about it. I knew something wasn't right.

Finally, that afternoon, my dad called. After my mom got off the phone with him, she was real upset. She gathered Patrick and me in his bedroom. We all lay down on his little twin bed, surrounded by four walls, each painted a different color—red, blue, yellow, green— and she started to tell us what happened.

"The reason your daddy isn't home—"

She paused. I could feel her body shaking as she tried her hardest to fight back tears. I was terrified.

"What is it, Mama?" I asked.

"It's because your Aunt Leelee, and Robin and Trent, they—they are now your angels in heaven."

I couldn't understand it. I was so confused.

My MawMaw was now my angel in heaven. I was sure of it. I remember my dad getting the phone call in the middle of the night. It woke me up. It was just after Christmas, and I had especially picked out a holiday figurine for MawMaw, a grandma angel holding a young girl. When they told me she'd died, my first question through tear-filled eyes was whether she got to open my present before she went to heaven.

"She opened it the night before she died," they told me. So even though I was so sad that I wouldn't see my MawMaw again, I had my pink "silky" that smelled like her—a special fabric that she let me pick out from her trunk of sewing scraps—and I had the belief that she was my guardian angel, always watching over me, just like the grandma angel I'd given to her for Christmas.

"What do you mean, Mama?" I asked. "Robin and Trent and Aunt LeeLee can't be angels in heaven. MawMaw's an angel in heaven. *What do you mean?*"

"They're gone," she said. "Honey, they're gone."

"How can they be gone?"

My mom clearly didn't want to answer me, but I would not stop asking questions. So she finally explained as best she could: "A bad man came to their house and hurt them," she said. "God didn't want them to hurt anymore, so they went to heaven where they could not feel it."

My mom started sobbing. Patrick cried, too, even though I'm sure he understood even less than I did. He's told me he has no memory of that day, and hardly any memory of the whole thing. But I knew something was wrong. I knew it when Daddy didn't come to my recital.

My mom wrapped her arms around me and Patrick, and we all sobbed together there on that little bed for a very long time. I stared out the window through my tears, staring and staring at the sky. I was waiting to see them, hoping to see them swoop down from the clouds.

It would take a few days for me to understand that Aunt LeeLee and Robin and Trent had been murdered. It would take months after that to put the pieces together, since nobody wanted to talk about it. And it would take years for me to get the whole story, once I was old enough to look it all up for myself on the Internet.

The murder of a mom and two young children, in their own home, in a quiet small town, was big news in Alabama. We occasionally saw flashes of the story come up on the news when the investigation was going on, and later when the trial was going on, but my parents always changed the channel. They couldn't take it. And clearly they wanted us to forget about it, too.

But I couldn't forget. Even though it scared me, I wanted to know more. It's just how I am. I remained silent and blocked it out for quite a few years, but I eventually found the strength to google the case. And the clearer and clearer the story became, the more horrifying it was.

One day, a man knocked on my aunt's front door. My uncle was at work. The kids were playing in the house. There was no school that day because it was a bad-weather day. My aunt was busy in the kitchen, but she went to the front door and answered. It was someone she knew. Someone she thought she knew well. A man who had done much of the remodeling on their house. A man she trusted. A man she and Uncle Stu had let live in their travel trailer in their backyard for weeks on end while the work was being done. A man they ate dinner with sometimes, in the kitchen where she was busy cooking dinner.

This man was out on a work-release program after being imprisoned for a nonviolent offense. My aunt and uncle had given him work. They had given him shelter. My aunt had sewn up the holes in his clothes. He was around so much and had so many conversations with them that my aunt considered him a friend.

So when he knocked on the door that day, she invited him in. Without hesitation.

No one can know what words were said, of course, because the only other people in the house were the kids. But from what he confessed, and what the police put together, my aunt stepped into another room for a minute to tend to the kids, and when she returned, she caught this man rifling through her purse—trying to steal money. His girlfriend was a drug user. An addict. She was desperate. *He* was desperate. He knew my aunt usually kept cash in her wallet, because it was from that wallet that she paid him on a regular basis. So he went there to steal from her. *Because he knew.*

When she walked back into the kitchen and saw what he was doing, she tried to stop him. He panicked. He couldn't take the thought of going back to prison. So he pulled out a Leatherman, a multipurpose tool, and stabbed her with it. Aunt LeeLee fought him off and ran into another room, screaming for Robin and Trent to run and hide. Robin tried to leave but had trouble with the door. So the man grabbed her, pulled her inside, took a steak knife from the kitchen, and stabbed her with it. The blade of the knife broke off in her body, so he grabbed another one, and stabbed her again until she was dead.

By this time my aunt had somehow fled upstairs and managed to get Trent to hide in a cabinet where my brother, Patrick, and I used to hide when we played hide-and-seek.

When the man came upstairs, she asked him why he was doing this.

He had "gone too far now," he told her, and he stabbed her again. As she lay dying on the floor, he found Trent. He slid open the door to the cabinets in the hallway. He pulled Trent out, four-year-old Trent, and he killed him, too.

When it was all over, he went back and stabbed all three of them again, just to make sure they were dead.

When my uncle came home from work a few hours later, he walked into a nightmare worse than any of us ever could have imagined. And to this day, I don't think any of us, least of all him, can fully wrap our heads around it.

None of it made sense.

I knew something was wrong. Kids *know*. Even little kids. They sense things. They understand more than their parents want to believe sometimes. And when my mom told us that somebody had come into their house and "hurt them," it terrified me in the deepest parts of my heart. Like I said, I didn't know the whole story with all the details until years later, but coming that close to something so awful, so terrifying—it was a turning point for me. It changed everything. I was no longer living in the innocence of an untouched childhood.

I sometimes still question if I'm in a really bad dream. You see tragedies like this on TV, but it doesn't happen in real life. Now that I'm older, I can't imagine what that was like for my parents, to have to tell their six-year-old and four-year-old that their beloved aunt and cousins were dead. How could that be my family? Our life as we knew it changed after that. *Everything* changed.

After the murder, everybody from my dad's side of the family grew distant. We simply couldn't all be together, because that meant facing the void and emptiness that the tragedy had left behind. Holidays together, family gatherings of any kind—they just went away with that side of the family. They just stopped.

My dad was heartbroken, and distant, and resentful. He'd lost his baby sister. He had lost his mother just before that, and a best friend before *that*, and his father a year before *that*. He was so broken. His anger, I think, mostly came after this all happened.

My brother and I lost a future full of family memories and celebrations.

I no longer held the luxury all children should have, to live in blissful imagination and protection from the realities of the dark world we live in.

I'd lost my innocence.

I experienced something so traumatic at a time when I didn't even know what trauma was. As a child, it's impossible to understand or recognize the feelings you have. You just learn how to survive. But I was so scared. I started waking up in the middle of the night in a cold sweat, believing fully that someone was at the door to hurt us. I wasn't scared of monsters under my bed; I was scared of someone being in my closet, sneaking into my window, breaking through our front door to kill my family. Not a monster. A *man*. And it wasn't because someone showed me a slasher film before I was old enough to handle it. It wasn't because I stayed up past my bedtime and watched an episode of *Criminal Minds*. It was because the things that happen in those movies and TV shows happen in real life—and they happened to my family.

We had a long driveway to our house, and for years whenever I saw a car come up that driveway, I would freak out and scream for my mom. I didn't want to open the door. I didn't want *her* to open the door.

I experienced all sorts of disturbing thoughts and fears, intense sadness, and what I would later recognize were regressive behaviors. I grew increasingly clingy, and my parents needed to constantly reassure me that I was safe. I stopped going to sleepovers; I refused to go to summer camp, not because I would be homesick but because I was terrified of what could happen. What *does* happen. Bad guys aren't always the ones who get slayed at the end of the movie. They are people you know. People who knock on your door.

Throughout the rest of my childhood, bedtime was a big struggle for me. My mom had to go through all kinds of rituals to get me to calm down and close my eyes. Rituals that I hoped would keep us safe.

First we said our bedtime prayers: "As I lay me down to sleep, I pray the Lord my soul to keep, and if I should go before I wake, I pray the Lord my soul to keep and take, amen." If that sounds a little different from the way you're used to hearing it, it's because my mom thought that "if I should go" was gentler than saying "die" to two kids who'd now experienced the brutality of murder in their own family; and adding "my soul to keep" instead of just "to take" sounded gentler somehow, too.

The thing is, when I said that prayer, I *meant* it. I was living with the harsh fear and example in reality that I could die, because Robin and Trent had died. I knew how real death could be, not just when someone is old and has lived a long life, but when they're younger than my dad. When they're a family member. When they're cousins. When they're Robin and Trent. When Robin was the exact same age as *me*.

My parents didn't believe in therapy, so neither my brother nor I saw a therapist to help with any of this. We just dealt with it, as a family.

The prayer at night wasn't enough. Even though I loved God and believed that praying would keep us safe, I needed my mom to call in backup. I saw how Sleeping Beauty was protected by her fairies, and my mom said fairies gave mommies "extra fairy dust, to help little girls go to sleep." And every night after the prayer, my mom would throw the invisible fairy dust around the room to protect me and help me fall asleep to sweet dreams.

We also called on the help of dream catchers. I had terrifying dreams almost every night, and one day when I was at a little festival at school, I found out what a dream catcher was. I insisted I needed one to help the bad dreams go away, and my mom was happy to buy it and hang it up. But just one didn't seem to work. So we bought three.

I also started to look for dream catchers wherever I went. And when I saw one, I thought of my aunt and cousins, and how they were watching over me.

The only way to make it through all of this at such a young age, though, was to believe in something so much bigger than me. Without my faith in God, and in heaven, I'm not sure I would ever have slept through the night again. I still have trouble sleeping now.

A few years ago I was diagnosed with narcolepsy, which isn't the joke they make it out to be in TV comedy shows. It doesn't mean I fall asleep mid-conversation or plop my head on a table and go out cold in the middle of dinner. It means that even when I think I'm getting a full night's sleep, I'm not. I never get the deep sleep that humans need to feel fully rested. So I'm tired pretty much all the time.

They say the causes are biological. Maybe hereditary. But part of me can't help but wonder if it's caused by fear—if my narcolepsy is a direct symptom of the trauma of the murder itself.

I can remember the car ride up to the funeral, sitting in my booster seat next to my brother in his car seat, staring out the window at the desolate roads and green pastures as we made our way to Hamilton.

I can remember seeing their bodies in the casket. Just one casket. My aunt and cousins were buried together, with Aunt LeeLee in the middle, and Robin and Trent on either side of her, wrapped in their mother's arms. They were so pale. It was easy for me to recognize, even at that age, that they were no longer there anymore. It was just their bodies.

I had to believe: They were angels now. Up in heaven.

I didn't cry once at the funeral. I remember just staying very quiet and wanting to leave the whole time, because the bodies weren't *them*. To this day, if the song "One More Day" by Diamond Rio or Garth Brooks's "The Dance" comes on the radio, my throat closes up. Those were the two songs played on a slideshow of pictures at their funeral.

Even though we never talked about it, and even though I buried the memories so deep in my heart that it truly was forgotten, whenever those songs came on I was forced to remember what I lost.

As I got older, on a couple of occasions I tried to talk about some of this with people I cared about, but their reaction was like, "Wow, that's awful. I don't want to hear about that. That's just too much to handle."

Look, I don't blame people for having that reaction. You might even be having that reaction as you read these pages.

Yes, it *is* too much to handle. But that's the thing about trauma: it happens anyway. I didn't have a choice to "handle" it or not as a six-year-old girl.

When, in my teens, I toyed with the thought of opening up and speaking about it again, it took a lot of strength. But I got shot down then, too. And it hurt. It kept me from dealing with the pain, and discouraged me from telling the truth—which only made it harder for me to find any type of closure and move on with my life. Instead, I just stuffed all the feelings and memories of it down inside and tried to pretend like it didn't exist.

I know now that there are options for kids and families in these situations. There are grief counselors I could have seen, and groups I could have joined. I just didn't know it then.

I wouldn't begin to heal until I was in my mid-twenties, in the presence of a therapist. And until I opened up about it in this book, almost no one knew about it. So now, I'm just hoping that you, and anybody else who hears about it, will take this story and treat me gently with it.

CHAPTER 6

SOMETHING BIG

During my 2020 quarantine self-help reading spell, I devoured some of Glennon Doyle's writing. So did a lot of other people. Her book *Untamed* was a huge best seller. And one of the things she talks about is how after she'd broken free of her old life and found more of her true self, her own mother noted that she hadn't seen her daughter that happy since she was ten years old.

The thing that she didn't realize then but realizes now, Doyle writes, is that around ten years old is when children start to realize their roles in life. Whether consciously or subconsciously, it's at that age—around the fourth grade for most of us—when we first figure out that there are certain boxes we're supposed to fit into, certain lanes we're supposed to stay in, certain types of people we're supposed to be to fit in with the rest of society.

It's from that point that we begin the long journey of figuring out what we're going to do with our lives. Not just in terms of career choices, but in terms of relationships, marriage, having kids, and more. And it's at that point where some of our spark, our childhood dreams and boundless energies and passions, tend to get lost. Or if not lost, then certainly buried.

It was a pretty remarkable thing to read, because it rang so true to me. As I look back now, I know that something definitely changed in me when I was ten years old. The only problem was, I had no idea what in the heck it actually meant. And I'm still trying to figure some parts of it out to this day!

The thing that came to me when I was ten is that I wanted to do something big.

That's it. I didn't know what "big" meant, what it was, what it represented, but I kept having this deep-down feeling that I was supposed to do something big with my life. As if God had some big purpose for me.

Great, I thought. *What the heck do I do with that?*

Why couldn't my spark have been *I think I want to work in a hospital!* or *I want to get married and have kids of my own someday!* or anything even slightly normal?

Having this "big" feeling without any context or understanding of how a girl from Alabama goes and does something big with her life just left me with all kinds of anxiety.

The problem, I think, is that I was still trying to figure out how to be the good girl I wanted to be instead of figuring out what was okay for me to be *outside* of those expectations. I couldn't seem to separate the core beliefs I'd been taught in my childhood from what might be right for *me*—and that caused a lot of internal friction.

I remember one Wednesday night at church, the pastor gave a sermon, saying, "God has a purpose for you!" And later that night, after all of my mother's bedtime rituals were finished, the prayer said, and the fairy dust sprinkled, I began crying. Sobbing, actually. My mom sat down on the edge of my bed. "What is wrong?"

"Mama," I cried. "I just don't know my purpose!"

"Oh, Hannah," she said, brushing the hair from my forehead.

"I just feel like God has a purpose for me, but I just don't know it!" I cried. "I don't know what I'm passionate about that's going to be my purpose."

My mom was so sweet about it. "All right, baby," she said, brushing my hair back over my ear and telling me it was gonna be all right. "You do, you *do* have a purpose. Of course you do. But we don't have to figure that out tonight. You've got to go to bed. You have school tomorrow."

I have gone back to that moment so many times in my life, and that has been such an overwhelming fear of mine—not knowing what my purpose is or what my passions are to be able to fulfill God's wishes.

As a young girl I danced, and I was still dancing then, long hours, every day—but I knew it wasn't my passion. I liked to color, I liked art, but we already know what happened to that passion. Plus, it never felt like my particular talent, and it didn't feel like it was my purpose. I liked to play kickball. A lot of kids do. But I wasn't on a kickball team, and it definitely wasn't my passion. So what was it?

Oh, my gosh, I remember thinking. *I don't have* anything.

And that left me feeling like I was failing God.

Talk about anxiety! What could be bigger than failing God?

In addition to Oprah and Ellen, I would usually catch the tail end of *The Montel Williams Show* on TV when I came home from school. Once a week he had Sylvia Browne on the show, a psychic who claimed to be able to talk to the deceased relatives of people in Montel's audience.

Watching Sylvia tell these distraught families that their loved ones were still around left me so curious. Were Aunt LeeLee, Robin, and Trent around me, too? And if so, was there some way I could talk to them? Was there someone who could tell me that they were okay?

I thought about them all the time.

After birthday parties and celebrations, whenever we were given balloons to take home, instead of taking them in the car with us, we would let go of our balloons and send them into the sky for Robin and Trent to play with. Even though sometimes I really wanted those balloons, I thought that Robin and Trent should have them, because they didn't get birthday parties anymore. We'd stand and watch them float all the way up to heaven.

I asked my mom what heaven was, and if I really had angels, and if those angels were here, how would I know? I desperately wanted to believe I would see Robin and Trent, but the thought was also scary. If I saw them, would they be ghosts? My comforting thoughts were scary thoughts at the very same time.

Like I said, my family never talked about what happened. But my mom seemed eager to help with the balloon rituals and all the bedtime rituals, and she'd try to convince me that Robin and Trent were definitely angels. I wanted to dream about them, but instead my dreams were traumatizing. Even when I asked friends to sleep over at my house, I'd still need my mom to come lie in bed with me sometimes.

How is a kid supposed to figure out their place and their role in life when they believe that the world is unsafe?

Add to that all the bone breaking, and always getting hurt, and the embarrassments that just kept coming when I tried to express myself creatively, and it's a pretty upsetting story to look back on.

As a fourth grader, how could I even think about doing something big, when clearly that would mean stepping outside of the boxes and lanes I'd been told were "good"?

"Big" didn't necessarily fit into being a doctor, or a teacher, or a lawyer, but those were the things I'd been told were good and okay to want to be. How could I balance what I was capable of and what everyone expected of me with this "big" feeling that I didn't even understand?

I worried that being big would be more than I was ready to step into. I didn't want to fail—I still don't. I would take risks and then get told I was wrong. And it never stopped. I took the risk and went on *The Bachelorette* and was shamed for the decisions I made. I took a big risk and got engaged on TV, and got my heart broken.

Again and again I've been shown that going with what everyone wants, what's expected, and then failing at that is the worst feeling of all. It just feels terrible. And yet, jumping into the unknown? Doing something people don't seem to even recognize? How does someone do that? And how does someone do it well? Do it "perfect"?

Because of the image I projected, I was *expected* to do good. When I messed up, I never heard, "It's okay, we all make mistakes." It was, "Hannah! You know better!" At least, that's how I heard it—no matter what they said. Whatever it was, the expectation from others, and mostly from myself, was that Hannah Brown was "good."

When I was late for school, because my mom was late for everything, it *killed me*. You got in trouble for that. And I didn't want to get in trouble.

I still think of second grade. There was a dress code at our school, and we were supposed to wear skirts and shorts that were longer than our fingertips when our arms were fully extended, and any kind of shirt or top had to come down below our belly buttons and rest firmly on our shoulders, with straps that were no less than three fingers wide. My mom didn't care about those rules. "You're a child," she told me. "You wear what you want."

But I cared. I wanted to be good!

Still, there was a shirt from Limited Too that I wanted so bad. One shoulder of it was thick and looked like the American flag, and the other shoulder was just a spaghetti strap. It was a kids' shirt, and I saw a girl wear it to school one day—a girl in an older grade than me—so I begged my mom for it, and she bought it for me. I was so excited. I loved that shirt so much.

I remember walking into my teacher's wood-paneled classroom that day, with that old stuffy smell of a chalkboard and erasers, and thinking how cool my shirt was. But no sooner did I walk in than my teacher, with her bright red lipstick that was always smeared on her teeth, pulled me out into the hallway, stood me by the mural of the kids of all skin colors and various abilities all playing together, and sternly told me, "Do your fingers." I placed my fingers over the spaghetti strap, and it was clearly too thin to pass the dress code.

"That shirt is inappropriate," she said. "Go to the principal's office. Your mother will have to come and bring you a new shirt."

It wrecked me. I was *good*. I didn't do inappropriate stuff! *Inappropriate* meant bad. I wasn't bad!

The principal took one look at my shirt and agreed with my teacher's assessment. I cried so hard. They made me call my mom to tell her, through tears, what happened, and she drove right over to the school. It's funny, but my mom, who could be so submissive and vulnerable to my dad, was feisty everywhere else. She came in all mad and upset about what this teacher and this principal had done to her daughter. "She's in second grade! How is anything inappropriate on a second grader?" she asked. "This is ridiculous."

Rather than bring a change of clothes and send me back to class to be further humiliated, she took me home.

I never wore that shirt again. Ever. Anywhere. To playdates. To the roller rink. Nowhere.

The older girl wore that shirt to school again on other days. I saw her! But in second grade, I was singled out and shamed for wearing that same shirt.

What was it about me that inspired that kind of negative attention for what I was wearing, which was nothing more than clothes that I loved, when other girls could get away with it just fine?

As I got older, I continued to dress well, and guys gave me attention because of it. I swear the teachers would *always* check me: "Put your hands down and make sure that skirt is past your fingertips."

It always was. I did the fingertip check at home. I didn't *want* to get in trouble. I wasn't like, "Let me see if they catch me!" That wasn't me. But I always got treated as if I was.

By age ten, when life is supposed to start to be all about the coming change into adulthood, and defining who you want to be, and pushing the envelope, I felt pushed more and more into the idea of conformity to avoid any kind of shame or embarrassment.

I desperately wanted to fit in the box, even though I had this deep-down feeling that the box wasn't meant for me. And that caused me constant conflict, constant friction, internally. My stomach would tie up in knots.

I was anxious all the time. Both Patrick and I had nervous stomachs. We were worrywarts, as my mom liked to put it. Was all my worry a result of the grief I swallowed at such a young age? I mean, I would cry on the way to school. I was so worried something would happen to my mom. I would be scared if she was in the bank too long, or didn't answer the phone. I kept thinking, *What if somebody took my mom?*

I'd even say it to her sometimes, and she would say, "Don't be silly." It wasn't silly. I had a constant fear that somebody else I loved was gonna die. The fact that my mom and Aunt LeeLee were around the same age, too, was more proof to my elementary-school mind that it could have been us who got killed.

But I think a big part of my nervous stomach was anxiety brought on by all of this inner conflict.

My mom never brought either of us to a doctor or therapist to do anything about our anxieties. I don't think anybody ever talked about anxiety disorders back then. But she did say a prayer for us in the car on the way to school every morning. We were both so nervous and anxious about the school day, and she would ask us, "What do I need to pray for y'all about?"

Of course, she did this while she was running late on the way to school, which made me even more nervous and anxious than I already was.

"I'm nervous," I would say. And she would pray that my nervousness would go away before I walked into school. It didn't. Only nobody knew, because I would hide it under my smile and my good-girl image. I worried about everything. What if I did my homework wrong? What if I forgot my homework? What if something embarrassing happens? It was upsetting to me that my mom's prayers didn't seem to work.

When I think about it, this worrywart feeling goes all the way back to kindergarten, when we were playing tag, and a bunch of us went into this little clubhouse thing, and this one boy looked over at me and said, "Your fly is unzipped!"

That crushed me. I went off in the corner and swung on the swing by myself, embarrassed. I'm twenty-seven years old and still remember this!

I was suffering from an undiagnosed anxiety disorder and never knew it.

*

As I got older I kept praying and praying, asking God to show me what my Big Purpose might be. I would close my eyes tight when I prayed, and you know what popped up? Truly, all the way through my college years? A screen. Like a TV screen. There was nothing on it. Nothing I could see clearly, at least. But it was absolutely a screen of some sort.

"What does that mean?" I prayed, and He never gave me an answer.

It seems ridiculous, right? Me saying this after having been on TV? But I don't feel that being on *The Bachelor* and *The Bachelorette* and *Dancing with the Stars* is my big. Not at all.

My big is something bigger than that. Different from that.

The more time I've spent thinking and reading about it, the more I've come to discover that lots of people dream of a purpose in life that doesn't fit into a certain box. And I think we need to start talking about that. A passion or a purpose can be *so* much more abstract and different than we think. Feeling a call to some purpose doesn't necessarily mean that you're going to be a preacher. It doesn't mean you're going to be a teacher or a doctor or a lawyer or a banker. None of those things added up for me.

There were times when I thought I wanted to be a doctor, and times when I thought I wanted to be a teacher, too. But what I really wanted was this feeling of something big.

And then I would feel bad when I said it, or even thought about it. Who was *I*? It wasn't that I thought that the other professions I've mentioned weren't big. They are! Is there anything bigger than a teacher's influence on generations of children? Or a doctor's power to save lives? Of course not. But my big wasn't that. It wasn't anything I could put my finger on, or anything I could see in my immediate surroundings.

I had never seen the sort of big I was dreaming about in the moms of any of my friends. And I felt the conflict of wanting to be one of those moms and wives, too. Where were the women who made big dreams come true, but who were also moms and nurturers? The fact that I didn't see them in my own world made me wonder if thinking big wasn't something I should do.

Plus, as Glennon Doyle and others have pointed out, girls are pretty and sweet. Boys are the hustlers, the go-getters. Boys *do* things. With girls, it's always about *how* they are. Girls are described with adjectives, not with anything about what they do. It's always "She's so pretty!" versus "He's so hardworking and strong." How could I not pick up on that and believe it to be true? It happened all the time!

Don't get me wrong: I wanted to hear I was pretty. But I also wanted to know that it was okay to *do*. "She's feisty!" "She's aggressive." "She's ambitious!"

As I turned the corner into middle school and high school, one big way I saw girls expressing ambition was through beauty. I also saw how some girls got out of Alabama and went on to bigger things through the Miss America Pageant. So beauty would become about ambition for *me*.

In high school, I would become "Miss Everything." I would get good grades, win awards, become homecoming queen—all on my way to something "big!"

The thing is, there was something else tied up in all that ambition. I was seeking approval: big, concrete, tangible approval from others so that I could feel worthy, happy, loved. And I can't help but wonder now if my need for approval is actually some kind of good-girl syndrome, in a more clinical sense.

Is my need for approval and achievement and recognition a type of addiction?

Given everything I've been through, and everything I've struggled with, there's this repeating pattern of me trying and trying and trying to be the best—to be perfect. As if whatever I was doing wasn't enough. And as I grew older, my need for approval followed me straight into my relationships with boys: "You like me, right? You like me?"

I came to rely on their approval, my parents' approval, my peers' approval, my teachers' approval, and more, however short-lived, to tell me that I was good enough.

But the real problem, the one I'm working on, is that *I* don't actually believe I am.

That's a lot to swallow, isn't it? A lot to understand? It's definitely a lot to me.

I guess that explains why staying on track has been like driving a *Mario Kart* course or something for me. There are just so many obstacles and distractions and traps along the way that keep trying to knock me off the road, and the trick to getting to the finish line is just trying to figure out how to stay on the track.

The thing is, I've been knocked off track a lot. And I realize now that one of the reasons for that is because so often I've either lost touch with or just plain forgotten about one of the most important safety features we're given as we drive through life. Too often I've let go of the faith that grounds me. I've forgotten that there are always angels right there at the ready to lift me and put me back on track, even when I've fallen off the edge.

CHAPTER 7
Guard Your Heart

*I*n fifth grade, my stomachaches grew worse. My mom seemed to think it was just my nervous stomach, and she prayed about it on the way to school every day, but the pain didn't stop. And it *hurt*.

I was also having trouble going to the bathroom, to the point where my mom took me to the doctor. They diagnosed me with irritable bowel syndrome (IBS). They suggested I eat more vegetables (I did) and get plenty of exercise (I danced every day and played outside all the time). But the pain didn't stop.

On school picture day, I'll never forget how I couldn't go to the bathroom, no matter how hard I tried. I was doubled over in pain. It hurt so bad it left me screaming and crying.

The school nurse suggested I needed to see a gastrologist, and my mom made me an appointment. But he said it was IBS, too. My regular doctor reconfirmed it and suggested more changes to my diet.

But I could barely go to school after that day. When I did, I'd have to stay in the nurse's office the whole time.

Finally my mom pressed it: "No," she said to my doctor. "There's something else wrong. Something worse. I know there's something wrong with my daughter."

They finally scheduled me for an MRI so they could take a look at my whole abdominal region and see if anything showed up.

It did.

They discovered a tumor the size of an egg on my pancreas.

At eleven years old, I had an egg-size tumor in my body.

They sent me for a biopsy, and a day or so later, my dad got a call with the results—not from our regular doctor, but from an oncologist.

The tumor was malignant.

Cancer.

Pancreatic cancer—one of the deadliest forms of cancer there is.

There was good news, they said. (Or at least, that's how my parents relayed it to me.) "They said the cancer is completely encased in the tumor," my parents told me. "It hasn't ruptured. Which means the cancer hasn't spread anywhere. It's contained. And if they get that tumor out, you'll be fine."

I didn't really understand what any of that meant, and I could see in my parents' eyes that they didn't fully believe whatever it was. They were *scared*. The funny thing is, I wasn't.

It's so hard to explain how, but I just *knew* deep down that I was going to be okay.

I knew deep down that God had a plan for me, even though my purpose was still to be revealed.

Like I said, we didn't go to church regularly as a family. We didn't say grace over every dinner. After his sister and niece and nephew were murdered, my dad withdrew almost entirely from any sort of churchgoing or prayer. After encountering something so awful up close in his family, I think he questioned how there could even *be* a God who would allow such a horrible thing to happen.

I did the opposite. I started praying a lot more often, and not just at bedtime.

I didn't talk to Jesus about what happened to my family with any kind of specifics. But I prayed for Aunt LeeLee, and for Robin and Trent, and prayed for God to protect our family from bad people. I still felt scared a lot of the time, and still had trouble sleeping, but I clearly found a lot of peace and connection to Jesus through those prayers.

On the day of my surgery, I wasn't scared about what was going to happen to me. At all. Even though my mother was in tears and my dad looked as worried as I'd ever seen him in my life as the nurses came to wheel me into the operating room, I looked up at my mom from my hospital bed and said, "Mama, I'm going to be okay. I know Jesus has me."

I was *sure of it*.

I was lying there in my pretty gown, which matched the gown worn by my new American Girl doll, Elizabeth, the one with the long blond hair who kind of looked like me; the one my parents bought me as an early Christmas present before the surgery. And I said, "Jesus has me."

My parents were really freaking out, and I couldn't understand it. I was just ready to get that tumor out and stop feeling bad. So in that moment, on my way into surgery, I somehow became the one who comforted my parents instead of the other way around. That's how strong my faith was when I was eleven years old.

How powerful is that?

No matter what you believe, or how you believe it, being grounded in something that you're absolutely sure of is powerful. Not only is it powerful for you, but it rubs off on the people around you when you share it with them, whether they believe the same way you do or not.

I was so sure that Jesus had me that the only thing I worried about all day was that I might lose my hair. There was a chance we'd have to go through radiation and chemotherapy, they said, depending on what the surgeon found once they got me into the operating room. But miraculously, I didn't need either one.

The doctors managed to take that tumor out entirely encased. It had splenic tissue on it, which means that I might have been growing a second spleen, which is just the weirdest thing. But they were confident that no cancerous cells were left behind after the surgery.

I had to go to checkups a few times for a year or so after that, but nothing else ever turned up in my scans or in my bloodwork.

It gets even better. That year, before I got sick, was the first year I had gotten my Presidential Physical Fitness award. In part because of all the dancing I did, I was fit. I had abs. At eleven years old! And I was a little worried that I'd lose that because of the surgery; that I wouldn't be able to do sit-ups and pull-ups the same, or might be left with a big scar on my belly, which everyone would see in my dance outfits.

But none of that happened.

My doctor, Dr. Harden, was amazing. He managed to do that whole surgery and get that tumor out through my belly button, so I wouldn't be left with any kind of big incision scar at all. If you look closely at certain pictures of me, you can see that my belly button is kind of twisted up and there are four tiny incision marks on my stomach. He had the foresight to say to my parents, "I'm not cutting this child open all the way."

He got the tumor out. And I was *fine*.

But it gets even better than that.

You never know what God has planned, and how what you're going through might be a part of His plan.

Earlier I mentioned that I had the best babysitter, ever: Casey Rae. I also mentioned that she was going to school to become a nurse. Well, after watching me go through this cancer scare and supporting me as I went through surgery, Casey was inspired to change her focus. She decided she wanted to work in the oncology unit for pediatrics, and that is exactly what she is doing to this day! She spends her days saving children's lives, and she's a warrior for these kids. She's the exact same wonderful caregiver she was for me for all of her patients now. She lives her life for other people and impacts people in so many positive ways. Who would've ever imagined that something as scary as cancer could be something that inspires another person to change their career, and then touch so many people because of it?

After going through all of that, I basically became our family's spiritual leader. I tried to get them to say grace at every meal. I got my mom to take Patrick and me to church regularly on Sundays, and Wednesday nights, too. My mom started teaching Sunday school, and eventually my dad started coming along with us.

In middle school I attended youth group and started carrying notebooks into church, writing down what the pastor said and my thoughts about the sermons, and how they lined up with what I was feeling or what I was going through at home. I guess that's really where I first started journaling, even if it wasn't the standard kind of journaling, like keeping a diary, that people think of when they first hear the word.

But keeping church as a regular part of my routine wasn't easy. The older I got, the more I got into competitive dance, and a lot of those events started happening on Sundays. That cut into my church routine. Wednesday practices would become much more important, and that would cut into my youth nights, too.

Pretty soon dating, and beauty pageants, and the self-imposed pressure to keep my grades up, along with my dedication to winning and projecting the image I wanted to project, all seemed to get in the way of my devotion to God. Praying and writing down sermons seemed to take a back seat to everything else.

Given some of the troubles I had in my high school years and beyond (which I'll talk about in the upcoming chapters), I wish I had put my faith ahead of all that other stuff. Maybe it would have given me more peace, like it did when I was eleven. And that's something I've thought about more and more in these last couple of years.

How much easier would all the difficult periods and circumstances of my life have been if I had walked into them with the simplicity of knowing that Jesus *had* me?

✳

It's hard to stay there, isn't it? It's just so hard to hold on to that.

That sense of peace that my faith brings is so great, and yet, as a teenager and even more so as a young adult, I've found that I'm only able to get waves of it. I struggle to give in to it and fully trust it.

Why?

Why is it such a struggle, when I know that I'm better off when I feel the peace of the Lord on me? Why do I struggle to remember the power of faith when I'm freaking out and going through all sorts of things in my life that are painful or uncomfortable? Even in the middle of those moments, I know way back in the back of my mind and deep down in my heart that I'm going to be okay—because Jesus has me. But it sure doesn't feel like it sometimes!

Oftentimes when I need faith the most, I find myself turning away. I get so busy with all the craziness of life that I sometimes just plain forget to spend time with the Lord. Or "I'm just so tired," I'll tell myself. "I haven't slept. I just want to sleep! If I did a devotion right now, I wouldn't be all in."

In life, I know I'm an all-in kind of woman. So if I can't be all in, I think, I'm just not going to do it at all.

I do that even though I know it'll cost me.

The thing is, ever since middle school I've had this relationship with the Lord. It's real. I can talk to Him, like a dad or a friend. And to have a personal relationship with Him is something a lot of people struggle with, especially if they were raised in the structure of a church. A lot of people don't even know what it means to have a "relationship" with the Lord. For me it's always followed that simple, almost childlike faith that I mentioned. In this case I see the Lord almost like a second dad.

Viewing Jesus as a father-figure presence in my spiritual life was just so powerful to me—a father figure I could talk to, and share my feelings with, and pray to, asking for help, asking for forgiveness, and receiving his grace and warmth in my heart.

It seems like it should be such a simple thing: to spend a little time each day with God, either reading the Bible, or praying, or just listening; not listening for some booming voice from the sky, but trying to pay attention to the inner voice that tells you what's right and wrong.

Yet there are too many times to count when my relationship with God has taken a back seat or just fallen off my radar for no apparent reason. There are times when I've gone and silenced His voice, too, when I felt in my heart that I was doing something I knew wasn't right, but I told myself, *I don't have time to listen to that. I just need to do it and get on with it!*

I can't tell you how many times I've done that and wound up going through something really hard, only to be afraid in the aftermath to go back and even pray about what'd gone wrong. Almost like I was embarrassed that I ignored Him, and so I just didn't want to bring it up. Like, "Oh, can I come back? Or is he gonna be mad at me?"

Why did I do that?

God isn't like a "Dad" dad. He wasn't gonna ground me. I know that God wants the best for me, which makes it so frustrating that the times when I've needed Him most are some of the times when I've pushed Him away; when I was so busy and under so much stress that I just couldn't make time for Him, couldn't take time to focus on my faith.

What a mistake that's been.

I can tell you I'm trying to get better. I'm working on it. I've written down my goals and intentions in life, and improving my relationship with the Lord is right up there at the top of the list!

But as you're about to see in these next few chapters, as I went through my pageant years, and figured out my relationships with my very first boyfriends, and fought a severe struggle with depression, and carried all of that straight into my time on TV, I had a hard time keeping the Lord *anywhere* on my list, let alone at the top. I struggled *hard*.

How crazy is it to think I might not have had to struggle quite so hard these last few years if I'd just let my faith be a part of my life, no matter where life happened to be taking me, or how embarrassed I was by the mistakes I was making along the way?

Why isn't keeping the faith a much easier habit to maintain than it is?

Speaking for our generation, I think there are times when we push faith away out of this mistaken idea that we're protecting ourselves by doing so; as if trusting in God and letting God in is something to be scared of.

That seems ridiculous, right? But hear me out: our lives move so fast, and we're dealing with so much all at once, that if we slow down enough to check in with ourselves, we might just come to realize that we're living in a way that doesn't serve us. I think some of us (especially me!) put up walls, like a defense, to the whole idea of faith, because we know, in the middle of doing things that don't serve us well, that if we listen to God (or Buddha, or the Universe, or whoever it is that you believe provides you with that inner voice you hear when you're real quiet), we just might have to face the results of our own actions.

What I'm saying is that if we take the time to talk to God to check the alignment of our actions with the knowing that's in our hearts—the right and wrong and inner peace that we all sense and long for, on some level, deep within ourselves—we might hear some truths that won't be easy to hear. And we might decide we have to change the way we're doing things. And change is hard!

Does that make any sense?

I know it's confusing, because it's been confusing for me.

I shouldn't be guarding myself against the Lord. That's exactly the opposite of what I should be doing. And I know that. I should let the Lord in to help guard me from everything else.

And even *that* can be confusing.

The whole question of who to let in and who to keep out in life is a big one.

I remember I took a weeklong trip to the beach for church camp in middle school, and at one point the pastor gave a sermon about "guarding our hearts."

"Guard your heart in Christ Jesus!" he said.

I opened up my Bible and looked up that passage, and highlighted it, and put a sticky note on it. It's Proverbs 4:23–27:

> *Above all else, guard your heart, for everything you do flows*
> *   from it.*
> *Keep your mouth free of perversity; keep corrupt talk far from*
> *   your lips.*
> *Let your eyes look straight ahead; fix your gaze directly before*
> *   you.*
> *Give careful thought to the paths for your feet and be steadfast*
> *   in all your ways.*
> *Do not turn to the right or the left; keep your foot from evil.*

I still use the same Bible today that I took on that trip. It's a pretty little Bible with a flower on the cover, but the spine is broken, and it's tattered and dog-eared. It's almost like this Bible is my relationship with the Lord in physical form.

I took that sermon to heart the moment I heard it, and right next to that passage in my Bible I wrote "Beach Blast '10!" so I'd never forget where I first read it. But then, for some reason, I forgot about it. For a long time I forgot. Just these last few years, in my relationships with men both in public and in private, I've gotten mad at myself on multiple occasions—*Man, you didn't guard your heart!* To be honest, it seems like whenever I've opened up my heart to people in recent years, they've destroyed it.

But how do we make sense of all that in the context of keeping our relationship with the Lord?

There are times when I've thought I never should have let those people in. I shouldn't have let *anyone* in! But that's not what the sermon was saying. I looked at it in black-and-white for a long time, as if we had two choices: guard your heart and don't let people in, or don't guard your heart and let them in.

When I was on *The Bachelor* and *The Bachelorette*, I didn't guard my heart. I opened up. (And my heart was already broken at that point, which you'll hear more about in just a bit.)

Being vulnerable and a little outside your comfort zone is where you find love, of course. Dating experts always tell you that. But what the Bible tells us is that we also have to move slow and protect our hearts against intrusion from the wrong people.

Think of the heart like a castle. There are guards outside the castle, but that doesn't mean *nobody* gets in. The right people, the safe people, the trusted people are allowed in.

I think the word *guard* in the sermon could be taken wrong, as in, "Let no one in!" And when I interpreted it that way, I'd shame myself for letting people in.

I had to work through that. I had to realize that shaming myself doesn't help anything. Mistakes are normal. I'm still learning.

There are moments now when I'll say to myself over and over, "Guard your heart, guard your heart, guard your heart . . ."

I thought about it on *The Bachelor* and *The Bachelorette* all the time. The producers and every fan in Bachelor Nation would tell me, "You have to be open for this process to work!" But in my gut, it felt unsafe. I knew that I needed to guard my heart, but I didn't trust myself to know who to let in, and who to keep out.

I suppose that brings me right back to the man at the front door of my aunt's house. How can we know who to let in, when even those we know can hurt us?

When you have trust issues and you hear the words "guard your heart," how can you possibly know who to let in and who not?

It's a struggle I would carry for a very long time. A struggle I'll likely carry going forward, I'm sure. But as I headed into high school and college, I think it was twice as hard—because I had to learn a lot more about myself before I could ever learn how to discern what I saw in others.

CHAPTER 8

Dreaming of Miss America

So much happened in my life over the course of the next few years, I can't begin to try to explain it all at once. Over the next few chapters, I'm going to spread it out by topic, so I can try to make it all make sense to you—and hopefully make more sense to me! (Seriously, there was so much happening all at once, it was hard for me to keep track of it myself.)

But looking back, I see it more clearly now. And since so much of this period was marked by my participation in pageants, that's where I'll start . . .

I really thought I was going to be Miss America when I grew up.

We started watching the Miss America pageant on TV when I was really young, and as a little girl I would put on my mom's high heels and practice my walk during commercials. I practiced saying my name and waving to the crowd like a princess, and putting my hands up over my mouth in shock when I pretended to win.

My mother started me in dance class when I was two. I loved being onstage, but my dance instructors always seemed to put me at the back of the group. My mom never put me in theater or pageants, where the spotlight really shone on me, and I wanted to be on a stage like that.

Thankfully, in Tuscaloosa I could participate in pageants at school—and at my school, they were a really big deal.

There were school pageants every year, starting in the sixth grade. The format was simple: You had to walk onstage in a dress while an announcer stated your name, said what grade you were in, and shared three facts about you. While the announcer spoke, you had to hit your marks to stop and pose for a bit—right side, middle, left side—and then come back to the middle for a final look. That was it. Usually somewhere between thirty and fifty girls participated in each grade, in front of a panel of three or four judges, which usually included a city council member, a former beauty queen, and a volunteer mom.

My first year I wore a poofy ball gown with a white skirt and a black-and-white top, my hair pulled back in curls. I still had braces, my mom did my makeup, and with hardly any practice I won third runner-up.

For my seventh-grade pageant, I practiced my poses a little more. I wore a light-blue Cinderella dress, and we did my hair up with a curling iron in doo-doo curls. (That's what I call those long, swirly ringlet curls that you *think* look so pretty.) Looking back, my eyebrows were *huge*, and I still had braces, but somehow I still came in second runner-up.

In eighth grade I finally had my braces off and my first big-girl haircut, with layers. I wore my hair straight with a beautiful coral-colored dress—and I won!

I had always loved getting dressed up and making myself look pretty, and I really loved being up onstage. How cool was it that I could get recognized for doing things I already loved? This was clearly something I was good at, and because of my dance training, the walking, stopping, smiling, and posing was easy for me. But my mom didn't want me to do pageants outside of school. She wanted me to stick with dance, and dance practice left no time for much of anything else besides school and church.

At least, that's what she thought.

That summer, one of our family friends whose daughter loved doing pageants talked my mom into letting me do one, too. It was all last-minute, so in just a few days I came up with a talent, a dance I could do; they practiced an interview with me, so I would be ready to answer questions onstage, and they taught me "pretty feet."

"Pretty feet" is the way you stand to present perfect pageant posture, with the heel of your leading foot placed back toward the arch of your standing foot. It's slimming to stand like that, and it's also really stable so you're not wobbly onstage.

I didn't realize this pageant was a big deal, relatively speaking. The International Cinderella Scholarship Pageant wasn't all that big in Alabama at the time, but in places like Texas and California, it was huge. Demi Lovato and actress Tiffany Thiessen and other girls who've made it in Hollywood and modeling have gone through this pageant system. I barely had any time to prepare, but I went on that stage and did my best—and I won the local Alabama branch of the pageant!

All of a sudden I was appearing in parades as a pageant winner.

They asked me to show up at community service events while I started prepping for the big Cinderella pageant in Dallas, where I would compete against girls who had done this their whole lives; girls who would go on to become Miss USA, and even Miss America. And the top prize was a $10,000 scholarship!

It took up so much time, my mom was like, "What did we get ourselves into?"

It was all so new to me, I didn't expect to win, and I didn't. I didn't place in the Top 10 in Dallas, but I placed in the International Beauty category, and I won the Cover Girl award. All of these adults and officials at the pageant told me, "You should continue doing this. You just need to be a little bit more polished."

My mom loved that it was something that we could do together, and so did I. Everyone was so encouraging. How could I not do what they said? I decided that pageants would be my thing.

I entered the Miss Alabama Teen USA pageant, which didn't include a talent portion, and I placed second runner-up right out of the gate. I was so excited!

Next I signed up for the Miss Alabama's Outstanding Teen pageant, and in my very first year I made Top 10. *Top 10!* My first year! At sixteen years old.

I entered again at age seventeen, knowing that if I won, I would receive a full-ride scholarship to college. My mom got me some professional coaching. I worked hard. I practiced speaking all the time. I put together a whole new dance routine, even though I was sick and tired of dance competitions and had decided to quit so I could focus full-time on pageants.

I went into that pageant with high expectations. I had all sorts of encouragement from my mom and from some of the pageant organizers, and all of these people who told me I could win it. I was a natural, they said. I was meant for this! And I made the Top 10. I even made the Top 5!

But I ended up getting first runner-up.

I was excited and devastated in the very same moment. The girl who beat me, her mom had been Miss Alabama, and her sister had been Miss Alabama Teen. She was fourteen. I won the onstage evening competition, which included the onstage question, but she won the talent competition. She was very talented, and I just wasn't the most confident dancer. I'd been put in the back in dance class for a reason, it seemed. People in the pageant world told me I needed to get better at dancing if I wanted to win.

I didn't give up. I truly thought I was going to be Miss America someday. That was my dream. So at the age of seventeen, I started competing with twenty-six-year-olds in the pageants that fed into the Miss America competition.

It was a big leap to go up against girls who had a decade or more on me when it came to competing in pageants. But I did really well. I won Miss Tuscaloosa, which was what I needed to do to get to the state level, and I thought I was on my way to making my Miss America dream come true.

That's not what happened.

I wanted it so bad, and I worked at it so hard, that I made it to the Miss Alabama pageant the next three years in a row—and all three years, I failed to make the Top 10.

I couldn't figure it out. Why did I keep doing well and winning when I was younger? It seemed like the more polishing I got, the worse I did. I kept asking myself, *What's wrong with me?*

Everybody told me that pageants were a pay-your-dues thing. "Nobody wins until they've done it for four years or more," they said. "Pay your dues, pay your dues." Judges, organizers, and even some of the older girls told me, "You're beautiful, try again, you're still young." But year after year, I felt more and more beat down.

Maybe I would have received that message better at twenty-two, after I'd finished college and grown up a little bit. But starting at seventeen, it made me feel so insecure. My self-worth just disappeared.

For the statewide Miss Alabama pageant, all of the contestants have to go to Birmingham for a week of rehearsals and preparations. They put us up in dorm rooms, where they took away our phones. We were completely isolated. (Not unlike the conditions I faced on *The Bachelor* a few years later, though at least then I was in a mansion instead of a dormitory.)

In that environment, it was easy for the other girls to get inside my head. Instead of feeling confident about the choices I'd made, I would look left and right at what everyone else was wearing and think, *I don't like my outfit now.*

What I failed to recognize was that the more desperate to win I became, the more I changed myself to try to match what I saw as winning. Year after year I tried to copy how the winners dressed, how they looked, the way they answered their questions.

I watched girls getting ready for their interviews, carrying binders. I didn't have a binder. So I got up early and watched CNN and obsessively took notes to get prepared for world affairs questions. I got so stressed out about being asked, "What do you want to do in the world?" at an age when I truly didn't know.

I still loved getting dressed up. I loved looking beautiful. I loved serving my community. I loved being onstage. All of those parts were fun. Pageants were sometimes a beautiful and empowering thing for me. I learned so much, and the recognition wasn't even about the applause for me. Under those big bright lights, I could hardly see the audience. There was just something about being up there onstage that felt right to me. As if that was the place I was supposed to be.

What I did not love was the pressure.

After coming so far and getting so close to the top in the teen pageants, winning was the thing I was supposed to do—yet I wasn't even making Top 10.

The anxiety and self-imposed pressure was a lot. I just couldn't take it anymore. I had a lot going on in my life at the time. I was suffering from undiagnosed anxiety and depression (which I'll talk about more in just a bit), and the Miss Alabama competition was too much for me to take.

I didn't want to give up on pageants entirely. I'd dedicated so much of my life to it. It was my thing. So I decided to give it one more try in the Miss USA system, which requires a little less preparation, follows a different format, and has a different set of rules. It was just a little bit less-intense than the Miss America system.

I entered the Miss Alabama USA pageant with high hopes—and I didn't even make the Top 15.

I was crushed. I had worked so hard, for so long, believing very strongly that recognition and affirmation equals worthiness. I just wanted to be accepted—and couldn't get over the feeling that I had been rejected.

As I'll explain in the upcoming chapters, there was just so much going on in my life at that time. I couldn't take it all. So I decided I'd never do it again. That was it for me.

Pageants weren't my thing, after all.

CHAPTER 9

LeGS

Looking back on it now, I think the way women are judged in pageants and the way we're judged in life aren't all that different. That was a problem for me, because so much of my happiness came down to my desire for approval. My whole life I've wanted approval: from my parents, my friends, my teachers, boys, judges, audiences, perfect strangers, everybody. The problem with wanting people's approval is that when they don't approve, it hurts. And it's really hard to shake that hurt, especially when the disapproval has to do with my body.

By the time I was four or five, I would look in the mirror at dance class and notice that my legs were bigger than the legs of the girls beside me. I danced on competitive teams until I was nearly seventeen, and that comparison in the mirror never went away.

I would look at Limited Too catalogs in second or third grade and think, *I don't look like them.* Even then, because I was dancing, I had muscular legs and a bit of a booty. And it bothered me that my body didn't look like those girls'.

In pageants, my body was literally judged and compared to other girls' bodies, and instead of feeling good about the differences, I never felt like I was enough. I stressed out over the fact that I could never change this situation. Why couldn't I fix it?

Where did that pressure come from? I'm not even sure. It was always just there. I think a lot of girls feel it. It's a reflection of everything we see, everything we read, everything we're told.

But the one trigger I remember the most came just before I went into kindergarten. My parents owned a hair salon that was also a tanning salon and gym—one whole section of a shopping plaza. A guy named Chuck ran the gym. I was always around at that age, hanging out in the back room watching *Grease* over and over till the VCR stopped working.

Chuck had all these cute little college girls working out in there, and one day I was in the back mixing ketchup and mayonnaise to put on my sandwich. I liked to mix the two, which grosses me out now, but I loved it then. And Chuck came in and told me, "If you keep eating like that, you'll get fat!"

I never ate mayonnaise again.

Why did I even know what "fat" was? Where did that come from?

For dance class, I hated that my feet were wider than the other girls'. I had to go to special places to get my dance shoes. I looked at myself in those pink leotards we wore and noticed that my thighs touched. On other girls, the taller girls, the skinnier girls, they didn't.

I would hear the older girls talking, including one who grew up to be a model. She said, "The perfect legs are supposed to have three holes, one two three—I have it!"

I looked in the mirror. *Shoot, I only have two, one by my knees and one by my ankle.*

My American Girl dolls' legs didn't touch.

My Barbies' legs didn't touch.

The little-girl models in the Limited Too catalog—their legs didn't touch.

In later years we danced in booty shorts, like tight spandex. I hated wearing them because my legs didn't look like everybody else's in them.

For as long as I can remember, I'd been told that I had "thunder thighs." Older people in my family, older friends of my parents, would pick me up and talk about how heavy I was. I remember they'd say, "Oh, oh, oh!" as if it hurt their backs when they lifted me.

When I got into pageants, I can't even count the number of times I heard the same passing comment from people. *You're so pretty, but if you could just lose ten pounds, you would really see a difference.*

I tried. I really tried.

I've never been naturally skinny. I don't have those genes. I've always been fit, but I had to work at it, which means working out. I work really hard. But I also love ice cream, and I love pizza and hamburgers and french fries.

I don't think most people would look at me at any point in my ups-and-downs in pounds and think I was "overweight." But I could not ever look like the tall, skinny model-type I so desperately wanted to be.

So where did that leave me?

In a perfect world, I shouldn't have cared. Why should any of us feel pressure to fit into a category of body type? My body is mine, it isn't like anyone else's, and I should have just loved and adored that I was uniquely me. But instead, I was drowning in insecurity and a self-hatred of my own body. I had such a warped view of what my body looked like versus what I thought it was *supposed* to look like.

How is a girl supposed to make sense of the competing messages?

Even if I wasn't in pageants, given everything we see in magazines, and in movies, and on social media, how are any of us supposed to be able to think of our bodies as not being in competition with everyone else's? I tell myself all the time, "I'm *not* a model; I'm *not* a fit model. I just want to be healthy!"

The first time I went on a diet I was fifteen years old. I was in tenth grade.

I was following a pageant expert's advice, and what she told me was, "You can eat from morning till noon, as much fruit as you want. After twelve, no fruit, and you eat chicken and green beans for both of your meals. Then you can have some almonds . . ."

In the second week it was no fruit, two boiled eggs, chicken and green beans, chicken and green beans.

In two weeks, I lost sixteen pounds. I don't remember how I felt on that diet, but I got abs! My legs were still big, but my abs looked impressive.

That was my first-ever pageant with a swimsuit competition—and I won second runner-up. Everyone said how great I looked.

And as soon as it was over, I gained it all back.

It was never healthy.

You can't get into the pageant world without hearing about girls taking water pills. There were girls that all they would eat was hard-boiled eggs, all day. The body yo-yo was just a thing, and it was incredibly intense in the weeks just before and after a competition. But I'm not sure it's all that different from the way we're all encouraged to diet and try to look in our everyday lives. We treat our bodies as if we're in some sort of competition.

I've been out of the pageant world for more than half a decade now, and all of these conflicting messages still affect me to this day.

When guys say "You have strong legs," I don't take it as a compliment. I hear it as "That means my legs are too big."

When I'm working out, I gain muscle easily. My legs could be giant if I wanted them to be. But when I was super skinny, you could see the muscle better, because I was nothing but bone and muscle. And people *liked* the way I looked at those times.

I hate saying this, but a part of me *still* wants my legs not to touch. I wish my thighs were skinny. It makes me sad when I hear other girls say things like that, but I wanted that skinny-legged model look so bad, and for a time, I had it. I know it's unhealthy for me, and it shouldn't be what I think about. But I think a lot of girls think it, even if they don't say it.

Body image haunts so many of us.

I am learning to love the feeling I get when I know I'm healthy, and being grateful for that, and being comfortable in the body I have. I'm proud of my athleticism. I can keep up with the boys. I do push-ups and can (if being chased) run an eight-minute mile. If you challenge me to almost anything athletic, I will do it.

I wish that was enough for me. I wish I didn't have these conflicting feelings. And I'm trying my best to shed them—like a heavy coat that I don't need to keep wearing in the summertime.

Unfortunately, it's taking me a long time to shake it off. Maybe that's normal. I spent so much of my life receiving these messages, it makes sense that it would take a long time to shed them.

I had a director one time who emailed me a picture of another girl and said, "You need to look like this by orientation week." It was a photo of a girl who looked nothing like me, in a swimsuit. I was twenty at the time, so this wasn't all that many years ago.

Another girl's body.

You need to look like this.

It killed me. This director had years of experience at high-level pageants. She knew what she was talking about. She knew how to win. I was trying to do everything I could to follow her advice and her coaching.

I had been trying to follow *everyone's* advice on what to do to "win." I did the diets. I tried the workouts. I dyed my hair the color of a potato chip because my hair wasn't the same kind of blond the winning girls had.

But I just kept losing.

I would practice for interviews and let coaches decide what I was going to say. Directors decided what I was going to put on my paper-work when I entered. They told me which books I should mention, and how many achievements I should have. I joined so many clubs in high school so it could be written on a piece of paper. I know some kids do that for their college applications, but for me it was all for pageants. I basically let other people craft a story of who I was.

Is it any wonder I lost who I was?

Undoing the things we've learned, especially the things we don't like, takes a lot of time and effort, whether or not we think it should.

I mean, even when we think we're *over* things in life, sometimes we're not *really* over them, right?

Like when I said I had made up my mind to be done with pageants after I didn't make the Top 15 at Miss Alabama USA. That resolution didn't exactly pan out: I came back to the pageant world one more time, for some unexpected reasons, in the most unprepared way, just a year later. And part of the reason I did it was because I'd gone through a breakup with a boy.

Oh, yeah. *Boys.* I almost forgot: while all of this pageant and body image pressure was going on, I was also trying to make my way through high school and college, while dating and dealing with the rest of my life.

CHAPTER 10

Little Miss Everything

I didn't kiss a boy until I was seventeen years old.

It's not that I wasn't interested. I was interested from the first day of high school.

Brady was in my freshman Spanish class, and I looked over at him and instantly fell in love. I can't explain it. Just looking at him did something to me that I had never felt in my life. I went home after school that day and told my mom, "Mama, I think I met the boy I'm gonna marry."

I've never felt that again, with any guy—even on *The Bachelorette*.

The only problem was, Brady had a girlfriend. So we didn't date. We didn't date until our senior year. But right away I could tell he liked me, too.

His girlfriend hated me, and she let me know it. To my face. It was like *Mean Girls* on steroids, and it got ugly. She could tell there was chemistry between us, and her way of telling me to keep away from him was to do things like write "B*tch" in ketchup, on my driveway. And this was before Brady and I ever dated!

I didn't really want to date anyone my freshman and sophomore years anyway. I was just too busy with pageants, which meant I was busy trying to be Miss Everything.

I worked really hard. I made all good grades. I didn't drink or party. I had more reason than ever to prove to everyone that I was the "good girl," and being in pageants helped me with that. I had no choice but to be smart about who I hung out with and what I did, because I didn't want anything bad to ever get out about me. My choices in life were all about the way other people saw me, which I realize now isn't exactly the healthiest way to live. But it gave me this self-imposed pressure to not mess up, and I do not think that's a bad thing to have when you're a teenager.

Heck, I didn't have *time* to mess up! Like I said, I was in *all* the clubs and did *all* the things. I never had dates to any of the events because I didn't date, but I got voted onto the homecoming court my freshman year. Our class was somewhere around five hundred people, and only two people from each class make the court. I did the school beauty pageant, and I won that as a freshman, too.

What I didn't understand, what I didn't see, was what my peers thought of all my "winning."

When I came back to school for my sophomore year, when the homecoming court votes were happening that fall, a bunch of my friends turned on me. "You win everything," they said, "so we didn't put you in this year." Not only that, but I found out there was a whole thing going around the school with people saying not to vote for me. I never *asked* for people to vote for me! I genuinely thought that winning meant people *liked* me. That they accepted me, you know?

But the accolades and attention I thought were so important

ended up hurting my relationships and connections all over school. Suddenly I didn't have a lot of girlfriends anymore. Some of them were jealous. But I couldn't say it out loud, because calling people jealous makes you sound as if you think you're superior to them. And I *didn't* think that. I felt like an outcast. I got really nervous going to school, and I felt like I couldn't actually talk to anyone about what was going on.

I felt insecure pretty much everywhere and all the time, except when I was up onstage. Onstage, I was good. I felt like I knew what I was doing. Offstage? I wanted my girlfriends to like me, that's all. I could not understand it: Why would they not like me just for doing well at the things I loved doing?

By the time my junior year came around, I didn't really fit in anywhere at school. Not with the jocks, not with the band geeks, not even with the other "good girls" and smart kids. The only girlfriends I had were some older girls from church and from dance class, who went to different schools. And they were moving on to college now. I felt so alone. But I got voted onto the homecoming court again that fall, and I chose to see that as my validation. There had to be a lot of people who liked me, or I wouldn't have made it, right?

And then one of the most popular boys in school started talking to me.

His name was Tucker. He was a senior, and he was *funny*. I loved that. The two of us could banter like nobody's business, and I'm just a sucker for somebody I can banter with.

He was cute. He was cool. He was on the baseball team but also played golf. And as soon as we started talking, I liked him.

He knew I had never dated anybody, and he asked me to be his girlfriend, and we dated for all of my junior year.

Tucker was my very first kiss.

I know he sounds like the dream boy in a Taylor Swift song, and he kinda was. But in some ways he really wasn't.

Tucker was the jealous type, and he hated that I was friendly with other guys. It was innocent flirting, never anything else. But he didn't like it—and he let me know that.

He got real possessive, like if I went home because I had a lot of homework to do, he would get upset that I wasn't spending time with him. So I started spending more time with him, because I thought maybe that's what a girlfriend is supposed to do. I stopped bantering with other guys, because I didn't want to upset him.

And then he wanted to do a whole lot more than just kiss.

I was into him. I was. I could have made out with him for hours. I let him take my top off in the back of a car, and that was a lot for me. I was a good girl! But he would always push the line, and I would have to tell him to stop.

He didn't like that, either.

He knew how self-conscious I was about my weight and stuff, and I'd be there with my shirt off, asking him to slow down, and he'd look me in the face and say, "You're not that pretty."

One time he looked at me and said, "You're fat."

I tried to play it off.

"Shut up!" I said. "No, I'm not."

I *wasn't* fat! I was at a healthy weight when we dated. I was sure of it. But then when I got home and looked in the mirror, I saw what he saw.

Let me just stop right here to say this behavior is not okay. Looking back on it now, I can see that I should have spoken up about it, and I should have gotten myself out of that relationship at the first sign of his putting me down like that. But back then, I didn't think I could speak up. Tucker was popular. I worried that people wouldn't believe me. I worried that people wouldn't like me if I said I didn't like *him*.

Being with Tucker felt good some of the time. He could be so charming, and *so* fun. We had our own playlist, and we could have a blast just singing and dancing in our seats as we drove around town. But then in private he had this possessive side that was honestly scary. If I wanted to leave his house, sometimes he would stand in the doorway and not let me leave. We would get into these really crazy fights, then make up, and I thought that's what couples did. I didn't know any different.

But it was confusing, because dating Tucker made me more popular with some of the girls in my own grade. They were talking to me more, and that was something I'd really wanted.

A few months in, Tucker told me he loved me. I didn't say it back at first, but I eventually did. I thought I loved him, that this was love. There were just some bad parts, but we were mostly good. Everybody loved him! How lucky was I to be his girlfriend?

But then he'd say "I love you," and instead of waiting for me to say it back, he would insist: "Say you love me!"

"All right! I love you, okay?"

"You don't mean it. You don't mean it!" he'd yell.

"I don't mean it 'cause you're driving me crazy!" I'd yell back, and we'd get into a big fight again.

Because of the pressure he put on me, I did things I definitely wasn't ready for.

I never had sex with him. I'd been told my whole life that it's wrong to have sex before marriage. But if I didn't let him touch me some place that I didn't want to be touched, or if I didn't do something physically to him that he wanted me to do, he'd get all upset and say, "It's because you don't love me." Then sometimes, when I absolutely refused to do what he wanted, he'd say, "Well, if you're not gonna do it . . . ," and he'd threaten to watch porn, or sometimes turn it on right in front of me.

Once again, I know now that this behavior is not okay, and that all sexual encounters need to be consensual. I didn't really get the distinction at the time, but for anybody reading this: If someone you're with is pushing the physical boundaries you're comfortable with, it's not okay. What is okay is to stop it, and to tell someone about it.

When I got upset with Tucker, he made excuses for his behavior. He talked about his parents' divorce, and how his mom and dad had issues, and how sad and miserable he was. I swear he tried to make me cry sometimes, just to prove to him that I felt bad for him. And it wasn't like I didn't feel bad a lot of the time I was with him—I *did*. I guess I just thought that if other people at school thought we were a good match, then maybe it was all okay. I'd seen my parents fight so much I figured that the fighting was, well, normal. That it was just what couples did.

Just before the end of school, when Tucker took his senior trip to the beach, my family went on vacation to the very same beach.

It was on that trip that Tucker's private behavior suddenly became public. My dad saw Tucker grab me and yell at me through the window of the place we were staying, and he came outside and went nuts on him. "You do not *do* that!" he yelled, and Tucker practically bowed down. "I didn't, sir," he said. "I wouldn't. I'm sorry."

I broke up with Tucker, but that wasn't the end of it. He came over early in the morning one time when my parents were gone. Either the door was open, or he knew where the spare key was, and he brought me breakfast in bed—while I was still asleep. I woke up to find him sitting on the edge of my bed.

"Please just leave," I said. "Leave me alone!" I closed my eyes tight. "I don't want to see you. I need you to go."

He climbed on top of me and grabbed my face and physically pried my eyes open with his fingers. "You're being crazy!" I cried. "Please get away!"

Another time, after I thought things had calmed down, he begged me to come see him at his house, and I agreed—and it caused a whole scene in his neighborhood because he wouldn't let me get back in my car. I started yelling, then screaming, and his mother came out and said, "What the hell?" as if I was the one causing the problem, because I was drawing attention from the neighbors.

It was awful.

I wasn't thinking of Tucker's behavior as abusive. I would have never used that word. But after yet another fight, I told my mom and her friends all the things that had happened, and they were shocked. I didn't realize how bad it was until I saw them start to cry about it.

"This is not okay," they said. And I finally got it.

This was *not* okay.

I told Tucker that I didn't want to see him again. He still showed up randomly at times, and "just wanted to talk." And it wasn't until I started dating someone else that he reluctantly left me alone. Honestly, if he hadn't graduated that year and gone off to college, I'm not sure what would have happened. Tucker didn't want to let me go. And I was *scared*.

That's what was happening behind the scenes of my life when I started competing to get into the Miss America pageant.

I won Miss Tuscaloosa, the first step in the process.

That led me to become the youngest competitor for Miss Alabama that year, and the whole town rallied around me—which made things even worse for me at school. I found my validation in the winning. I tried to keep my focus there, in the only place where I seemed to be accepted. But I went into my senior year terrified that I might win homecoming queen, because if I did, I knew people were going to be pissed.

For homecoming court, it was just my class that voted. For homecoming queen, the whole school voted, and because of all the attention I'd had around town, the odds were in my favor, which is exactly what I did not want.

Oh, and as if to add insult to injury, Brady's on-again/off-again girlfriend, who had gone to another school during her sophomore and junior years, was now going to our school again. Which meant I had to face her scornful looks every time we passed each other in the hallways.

That October, at an assembly full of the whole school, it was announced that I had been chosen homecoming queen—and a majority of the seniors didn't clap for me. In an auditorium full of people, one whole section of my classmates sat silent.

It should have been a moment to celebrate, and it was awful. Since no one had asked me to homecoming, my little brother, Patrick, was kind enough to stand up there next to me as my escort. He kept patting me on the arm, saying, "It's okay, it's okay."

In the parking lot after school, just as I was getting ready to leave, Brady's on-again girlfriend walked over and spit her gum in my face through my open car window.

"That's what you get for being a b*tch," she said.

I sat there in shock as she walked away. I rolled up my window. What had just happened to me? What had I *done*?

*

People on the outside kept describing me as the most popular girl in school, but in reality nobody really knew me. Most Friday and Saturday nights I stayed home watching movies with my mom and dad. I wasn't invited to the parties; I wasn't asked to join the hangouts.

My life in high school looked one way from the outside, when in truth it was completely the opposite. And no one felt bad for me. I was "popular." I was the homecoming queen. Why would anybody feel bad for *that* girl?

But man, I was so lonely. And hurt.

And when people feel hurt, they tend to seek out something— anything—that feels good.

CHAPTER 11

Boundaries Matter

One of the only people who I really connected with during my senior year of high school was Brady.

Yes, *that* Brady. The boy I fell in love with at first sight.

He was in my history class senior year, and we started talking again. And flirting again, innocently. He texted me sometimes, about homework, or just to say hi. We hadn't talked, really, in years, not after all the drama with his girlfriend. Up until senior year, I'd basically avoided him.

It was the third week of October 2012. He and I were texting, late at night. Taylor Swift's new album, *Red*, had just come out, and I mentioned that I hadn't had a chance to listen to it yet.

Neither had he.

"Come pick me up," he texted.

"No way! It's too late. We'll get in trouble."

"Come on," he texted back. "Everyone's sleeping. No one will know. We can drive around and listen to it in your car."

I don't think he *really* wanted to listen to the album.

My heart was beating so fast as I snuck out of my house and pulled out of the driveway with the headlights off. I turned them off again as I pulled up to his house, and I texted him, and he snuck out, closing the door to his parents' house real careful so he didn't wake them up.

We whispered as we drove away, which was silly because no one could hear us from inside the car.

"Why are we whispering?" he said.

"I don't know!" I said, laughing.

We started talking like we always did, and then I put that album on and turned it up, and I swear that girl was singing about my life. Every album of hers seems to be that way, like they all come out at the perfect time for whatever's going on in my world.

After that first night, Brady and I just kept sneaking out together. At first it was just as friends. Flirty friends, like always. But then one night we drove out to his hunting property, and he made a bonfire, rigged up a radio, and we sat out there for hours listening to music and chatting. It was chilly, so I cuddled up right next to him, heart racing. And he brushed my hair behind my ear with his fingers, and we looked at each other, and we stopped talking.

It was a first kiss right out of a country song. And it was an A+ first kiss.

It was everything I ever dreamed.

I swear, either Tim McGraw's "Felt Good on My Lips" or George Strait's "Give It All We Got Tonight" came on the radio every time we were together.

Brady was still on and off with his girlfriend at the time. I never really knew if they were together or not, but I also didn't want to know, so it wouldn't make me feel bad. It would break my heart when I saw them holding hands in the hallway, finding out they were back on. I didn't want to be *that* girl. I never thought I would be the girl somebody was cheating with, ever! But it felt so good to kiss him. So wrong, but so good. I kept thinking, *Pick me. Choose me. Love* me. (Yes, I was a *Grey's Anatomy* fan.) Every time I thought they were broken up for good, I would get so hopeful. Maybe we really could just have a shot and give it a real go, instead of sneaking around, me waiting for those texts to come meet him. But that's what we kept doing. We met up in the parking lot by the Econo Lodge, near the Publix. You couldn't see where we parked from the street. It was all supersecret, because, well, he didn't want to be seen. And I didn't want to look bad.

That parking lot turned into our spot. It was close to both of our houses, so night after night we would sneak out, and meet up, and talk and make out with each other, for *hours*, in the back seat of his bright-red Ford F-150.

When I hear that old Bob Seger song "Night Moves," I think of Brady. We didn't go all the way, but in the back seat of his truck we would get pretty hot and heavy. Just exploring each other, so *fearless*. When I think to those days, I still smile. It was a little bad, yeah, but I finally felt like myself. When my mom found out just recently that her "golden child" had snuck out of the window, she was just floored.

It was that kind of young dumb love that makes you feel alive. During those nights, I finally felt like I didn't have to keep up the act anymore. I could be free. Free to not be perfect. Even though sometimes I had to breathe quietly while I snuck around, at least I could finally breathe.

I loved Brady. I didn't tell him that. I was too scared. I couldn't tell him when we were in secret like that. But I thought he loved me back. He told me he did. And it's hard to describe how good it felt when said it.

I knew he'd been sexually active. But he never pushed me. He never made me feel uncomfortable. He never made me feel bad for wanting to stay true to my values. That gave me a false sense of safety. And it's safety that I needed in order to be open, and so much more willing, if you know what I mean.

I knew it was wrong to be sneaking around. I didn't feel good about hiding this, or doing any of this behind his girlfriend's back. When it was clear that they were together, I wouldn't talk to him. I wouldn't go meet him. But, gosh, I wanted to be with him. I couldn't understand why he would go back to someone who was so mean to me. I couldn't understand why he *ever* picked her over me. Why did I feel the need to have to prove myself to him? Eventually he didn't feel good about it either.

Brady broke up with that other girl. "It's over. For good," he said.

We waited a little while before he and I went public, and then suddenly everyone at school knew we were a couple. We did *everything* together. Well, not everything. He had a separate life, a party life that didn't include me. But we did everything else. We spent time with each other's families. We went to prom together. He had already made up his mind to go to the University of Alabama, right there in Tuscaloosa (Roll Tide!), and so I decided to go to UA, too. Of course I never told anyone that he was the reason, but he was definitely one of the biggest reasons. (Girls, never follow a boy!)

Toward the end of our senior year, I was getting ready to go into the Miss Alabama pageant for the first time. I was feeling good about it. I was so prepared, and *so* into it. But my dedication to the pageant meant I couldn't go on our senior trip.

Brady was going. So was his ex. That made me nervous, and we talked about it. He assured me he had never been happier than he was with me, and had no interest in getting back together with her.

The night before they left, I snuck over to his house. He picked me up and carried me up the stairs to his bedroom. We just wanted to spend the night together, and we did. We snuggled in his bed, and nothing more.

That night, I finally whispered in his ear, "I love you."

"I love you, too," he said. "And I promise you have nothing to worry about."

I worried the whole time they were gone. He stopped really calling me during the week, and when he did, he sounded like he had been drinking. I made myself sick over it. I lost like eight pounds that week—not from dieting, but from worrying.

I heard from a friend that Brady and his ex had been hanging out together the whole trip. "They looked really close," the friend said. "Like, really close. As if they were *totally* back together."

Brady and I had told each other everything on our late-night escapes. He knew every detail about me, and what had happened in my relationship with Tucker, and probably everything I've told you about my childhood that you've read in this book, and so much more. I wanted to know everything about him, too. But I didn't. There were things he was hiding from me, and I wouldn't find those things out till years later.

So the first time we saw each other when he got back, I asked him, straight up, what was going on. And I trusted him. I expected him to tell me the truth.

He admitted that he and his ex had hung out. He said they talked. He told me that they still had a spark. I felt my heart sink, but I was kind: "I understand, y'all have history and will have a connection, but that doesn't mean that what we have isn't great and worth continuing to grow." I didn't want to accept the underlying truth.

"Well, did you kiss her?" I asked. "Like, what happened?"

"No. *Nothing* happened. But . . . I think I want to give it another try with her."

I couldn't take it. To this day, Brady would say he's never seen someone cry like that. I was so broken. I wasn't dramatic, I didn't curse, I was just heartbroken. This was two days before I left for the pageant I had been preparing for all year. Needless to say, I didn't handle it well. The heartbreak killed any chance I had at doing well that year.

✳

It didn't take long before the truth came out, and I was told that they had not only kissed, they'd slept together on that senior trip.

It felt like everything had been a lie.

Just a few weeks later, I ran into a guy named Luke. He was a year older than me, and he was a quarterback in college now. He was such a catch, and I had always admired him when we were growing up in town. We ended up having a fun summer romance. He helped me find my smile again. Luke was a class act, a good guy—and he let me know that he was all in with me at the end of summer. When I went to UA, and he went back to football, he wanted to continue our relationship. So did I.

Well, guess who was sitting in my freshman math class at UA on the very first day?

One look at Brady, and all those old feelings came rushing right back.

I told Luke about it, and he warned me not to go backward. "If you do, I'll be disappointed in you. You're better than that," he said.

I knew he was right, but Brady started texting me, and he just had me wrapped around his finger.

The beach has always been my happy place! And yes, I've always been messy.

With Mama on vacation.

"Snowing" in Alabama meant one flake of snow. But I loved it!

With my cousin, Robin.

First impressions of Patrick. I wasn't
so sure about having a brother.

An early Halloween, dressed as
the Cinderella bride. I insisted I
was going to marry myself and
have a big wedding party.

Me and Patrick with our dad and
older sister, Alisa.

My angels: (counterclockwise from
top left) Aunt LeeLee, Robin,
Trent, and MawMaw.

My first dance recital ever.
I hadn't quite mastered the
"soft smile" yet . . .

Mama always curled my hair
for special occasions!

Wearing the
American flag shirt
referenced in
chapter 6.

Doing a class presentation for the
Museum of Famous Americans. I did
my project on Shirley Temple, who
taught me how to love my dimples.

My best friend, Olivia, and I did *everything* together growing up. Our moms were also best friends, so we were basically raised like sisters. All my fondest (and fun!) memories are with Olivia!

This was my first ballet *en pointe*.

After competing in my first beauty walk at a school pageant.

My first official headshot as Miss Tuscaloosa. I was a senior in high school and devoted all my free time to preparing for the Miss Alabama pageant. I was seventeen.

PHOTOGRAPH BY CROSBY THOMLEY PHOTOGRAPHY.

During halftime at our homecoming football game, being crowned Homecoming Queen!

With my college roommates Katie, Madison, and Caroline. This was right after I broke up with Brady and these girls were an incredible support system.

With my family.

This was my birthday in college during my sophomore year. I had all these amazing friends come to celebrate with me, but I was really struggling with my depression and I remember feeling so guilty for feeling sad when I knew I was so loved.

My first time in California. I was there for an internship and had no idea that by age twenty-seven I'd be living near the Santa Monica Pier.

After battling some serious depression in college, I finally found solutions through medicine and renewed hope in God. My senior year, I decided to get baptized again to honor and declare how my faith in God got me through a hard time.

Graduating from the University of Alabama. I was actually kind of upset on this day because my boyfriend had just broken up with me, and I'd really hoped he'd show up to graduation. (He didn't.)

Preparing for the Miss Alabama USA pageant. I was incredibly sad after two heartbreaks, and I remember walking into this pageant dress shop and people telling me that "breakup skinny is the best skinny."

Winning Miss Alabama USA. I hadn't even placed in the top fifteen in years, so I was completely shocked when this happened. It had been a really tough year and winning meant so much to me.

As a pageant titleholder, I really wanted to be a mentor for young girls—and I took that responsibility very seriously. It was really important for me to be someone they could look up to and to serve my community wholeheartedly.

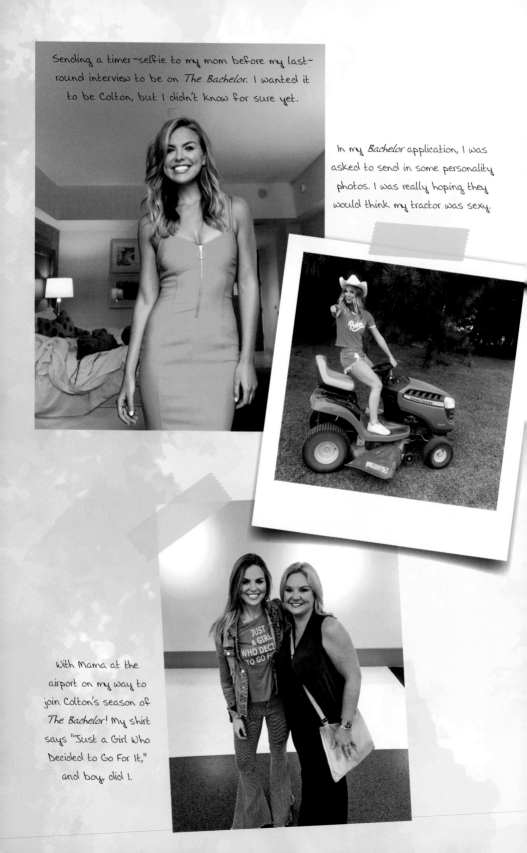

Sending a timer-selfie to my mom before my last-round interview to be on *The Bachelor*. I wanted it to be Colton, but I didn't know for sure yet.

In my *Bachelor* application, I was asked to send in some personality photos. I was really hoping they would think my tractor was sexy.

With Mama at the airport on my way to join Colton's season of *The Bachelor*! My shirt says "Just a Girl Who Decided to Go For It," and boy, did I.

On a group date in Thailand, Hannah G., Demi, and I went rogue finding food to survive in the wilderness.

PHOTOGRAPH BY JULIA LAPLACA

Heather and I twinning with roses and black dresses. A really fun night!

PHOTOGRAPH BY TODD SNYDER.

The night I got dumped from Colton's season. I had a burger, fries, and two milkshakes . . . and I definitely deserved it.

PHOTOGRAPH BY TODD SNYDER.

The day I found out I was going to be the Bachelorette!

During night one of filming for *The Bachelorette* with my main man, Sully.

PHOTOGRAPH BY SAM TAYLOR.

A behind-the-scenes shot while filming my trailer for *The Bachelorette*.

PHOTOGRAPH BY JULIA LAPLACA.

PHOTOGRAPH BY JULIA LAPLACA.

In Scotland on one of my favorite group dates.

In Amsterdam, after I'd told Peter I was going to go home and meet his family.

Trying to figure out if Tyler was my lobster. (Yes, I love Friends.)

In the very short post-engagement period with Jed.

After finding out what Jed had done, this is the photo I sent to a friend who asked how I was doing. I literally binge-watched *The Handmaid's Tale* and didn't get out of bed unless I had to for a whole week.

When things are really bad, Disney is always a good idea.

PHOTOGRAPH BY SAM TAYLOR.

♡ XOX

I've gotten to meet a lot of cool people, but for me, meeting Taylor Swift was my fan-girl dream come true.

This is what moving across the country during a mental breakdown looks like.

PHOTOGRAPH BY SAM TAYLOR.

Rehearsing for *Dancing with the Stars* with my partner, Alan. This dance studio was the closest thing I had to home at the time—I was definitely there more than I was at my own apartment!

PHOTOGRAPHS CARE OF MARLYNDA DO.

Right after winning *Dancing with the Stars*. Even though there was a moment of relief and a split-second of happiness after winning, I expected it to feel different.

After *Dancing with the Stars* was over, I found a new distraction in boxing—and I wound up really loving it. This is me with my trainer, Leyon.

I went back home for the holidays after *Dancing with the Stars* and wanted to help a family in need, since I had the means, by buying them Christmas gifts.

The night of Hannah G. and Dylan's engagement party. I had no idea what was going to happen that night, but it turned out to be beyond what I could have expected!

With Mama and Patrick in March 2020. I was home unexpectedly right before the lockdown.

Finding joy at my forever happy place.

New beginnings ahead . . .

I distanced myself from Luke. Things just fizzled out between us. I can see looking back on it now that it was a huge mistake. I let go of a really good guy just to fall back into the same old bad relationship.

Brady and I slowly but surely got back together. I tried to put everything behind me, but I couldn't stop thinking about what he'd done. I still wondered why he felt the need to go back to his old girlfriend when we had seemed so happy together, so *good* together, and the only thing I could come up with was the sex.

Did I need to start having sex with him? I wondered. *Was that what was missing?*

It's ridiculous, right? Looking back on it, I can see that I basically blamed a part of myself for his cheating, and then tried to make it right by pushing beyond my own boundaries. (Girls: Don't do this!)

When you're looking to other people for validation, the problem is, you'll be willing to bend your boundaries or break right through them to win them over. And the thing I'm slowly coming to realize now is that the more I establish boundaries, the better off I'm going to be.

But that isn't what I felt then.

I loved Brady. He said he loved me. I wanted him back, and I wanted him to stay.

At the time, it felt right.

A lot of people say their first time was terrible, or at the very least awkward, because they didn't know what they were doing. That wasn't us. We *knew* each other. We'd built up our desire for each other for a long time, and gotten to know each other from all those nights making out in the back seat. Our first time was two people who loved each other, and it was so sweet, and so pure, and even though it was sex out of marriage, it felt safe to me.

I'm a physical person. I'm touchy-feely. I love a good make-out session. But I don't want that to be all a relationship is. I'm not interested in sex without emotional connection. I'm not a prude at all, I'm just emotionally driven for physical desire—and my emotional connection to Brady was huge.

Our first time was the way you think it's *supposed* to be, which I think is really rare for a first time.

At the same time, a part of me regretted doing it, because I knew I wasn't supposed to. I was conflicted again, this time in an internal struggle of shame. *What I did was bad,* I thought, *but I'm not bad, and he loves me, and it felt right.*

At UA, while experiencing the freedom of living on our own, away from our parents for the first time, Brady and I kept having sex. A lot of sex. For about six months, and then I freaked out. It stopped feeling special. It almost just became something we did. It became a cycle. I mean, you can't have cake every day without feeling sick or guilty, right?

On Valentine's Day he bought me lingerie, and I was kind of like, "Oh. Okay."

It felt like he was looking at me as more of an object; looking at the lovemaking we shared as something more physical/sexual than the emotional/loving act I thought it was in the beginning. I also think the more we kept doing it, the more I kept internalizing my shame over having sex in the first place.

We started making out, and I stopped and said, "I can't do this anymore. This is not me. I love you. But . . . ," and I explained to him what I was feeling.

He said he understood. He said it was okay. But there was resentment from him. I could feel it. When we'd start making out after that, he would say, "You're teasing me." I wasn't trying to tease him. I was drawing a line in the sand—but we had already crossed that line, and that made it really hard to go back.

I kept pushing my limits, questioning, *How close can we get to that line before I feel bad about it?*

I also still carried the resentment of him cheating on me. Could I really trust him after that? The trust I felt wasn't automatic anymore. And I didn't know how to deal with that.

The two of us stayed together all the way through the end of our junior year. We didn't date other people. Everyone assumed we were on our way to getting engaged. The assumption was that we would get married sometime after college. That's just what people do from our neck of the woods, so I kind of assumed that's what we would do: take the next step. Especially since we loved each other as much as we did, and we'd been together for so long and gone through so much together.

By that, I mean Brady was there for me through some really dark days.

Our relationship happened over the same period of time during which I stopped having success in the big pageants I entered. We stayed together as I went through the worst of my weight and fitness struggles. But it was more than that.

When I got to college, which was just a fifteen-minute drive from my parents' house, I realized I didn't stand out anymore. High school had been challenging, but at least I had my pageant successes to let me know I was valued. UA was different. It seemed like there were two thousand other girls as high-achieving as I was. For a person who was always looking outside herself for validation and approval, that was really hard. I didn't feel special anymore.

I rushed the very best sorority, hoping to find a group of girls I would bond with, since I had never really had a group of girlfriends my age. I quickly discovered that they didn't usually accept girls from my high school. TCHS wasn't considered a "classy" school. They liked to take girls from rich towns, preferably those who went to private schools. They made it clear that I was an exception.

They kept reminding me of it, too: "You got in, but . . ."

But what? Was I supposed to get on my knees and praise them? Was I some kind of charity case? It wasn't right.

I got into that sorority thinking I'd achieved something, but then I didn't want anything to do with it. Brady wasn't allowed to come to some of the socials because he wasn't in a fraternity, and *that* was against the rules. We were encouraged to "get to know" fraternity guys. Plus, there was always a party going on, and we were expected to be at those parties. I drank a little at school, for a hot minute the first semester, but I always felt bad about it. So I stopped.

I realized that the sorority had accepted me for my accolades. Not for *me*.

Combine that with my body-image issues, my potato-chip-colored dye job, and my continued rejection in the pageant world, and I swear I didn't even know who I was anymore.

My whole life I'd been anxious about things, worried about whether I was doing things right, or doing the right things. Once I was in college, that anxiety tripled. Only now it was mixed with a feeling I'd never felt before.

In my sophomore year, I started skipping classes. I did my work. I still wanted good grades. I got upset if I got less than a 95 on a test. But I spent all day in bed. I didn't want to do anything. I didn't want to go anywhere. I truly felt like I couldn't.

I stopped going to church. Even when I went on an occasional

Wednesday night to get together with a group of peers and talk about our faith, I didn't pay much attention or really participate. I started drawing myself away from God.

I felt like I didn't know what my purpose was in school, or in life. I didn't *care* about my relationship with God. It was not that I was going and doing crazy things. It was just that I didn't care.

Brady was good to me. He would lie in bed and hold me and let me cry, and I'd tell him, "I just feel sad. Why do I feel like this every day?"

"Maybe you need to go see somebody," he said.

I didn't listen.

One day I dragged myself to campus, and I just started silently crying in the middle of chemistry class.

I tried to talk to my mom about it. "My life is gray. I don't have anything that's, like . . . I don't have a reason to be sad," I said. "But I *am* sad. And that makes me even *more* sad."

My mom basically told me to get over it.

"Everybody gets sad, Hannah," she said. "You're fine."

My mom had grown up with a mother who had tried to kill herself during most holidays she can remember. She spent Christmases visiting her mom at a mental hospital. She was mad at her mom for what she'd done, and I'm pretty sure she thought her mother had made a choice to be the way she was. Talking about depression, or, God forbid, any kind of mental illness, just wasn't something that happened in our house.

Plus, I looked fine. I wasn't doing drugs. I wasn't drinking. I wasn't hurting myself. And my little brother was acting out in all sorts of ways. My parents had their hands full with him.

"Stop talking about it. You're fine!" was the message they gave me. "You have no reason to be sad."

I went back to school and tried to be okay. But nothing got better.

That summer I couldn't even drag myself out to go to the beach. The beach had always been my favorite place to go, my favorite place to *be*. I used to tell people it was the place where I felt God's presence. "I just love the way the sun feels, hitting your skin. Staying out there all day. I don't wanna do anything else. I just wanna be on the beach!" That was me.

The one time my parents managed to get me to go with them that summer, it didn't help. I got to the beach and still felt this overwhelming emptiness and heaviness. Even with my toes in the sand, the tears welled up in my eyes.

My mom looked over at me, bawling in my beach chair. She of all people knew the beach had always been my happy place.

"We will get you help," she said.

After that, both of my parents were more compassionate with me, but I still didn't get myself to a therapist or psychologist. It wasn't until I got a routine checkup that our family doctor noticed something was wrong. He looked me over, checking my vitals, and then asked me directly, "Are you happy?"

I swear, it felt like no one had ever asked me that question before.

Huge tears welled up in my eyes, and it hit me: I wasn't just sad.

"No," I said. "I'm *not* happy. I don't remember the last time I was happy."

We talked about everything that I'd been feeling, and he put me on medication.

I didn't take it at first. I had all kinds of anxiety about taking it. I felt shame about having to take something just to help me feel good. I kept thinking, *Why am I like this? Why can't I just be happy?*

When I went back to UA for my junior year, there were three sorority sisters living in the house where I lived, and they noticed that I wasn't okay. They saw me—really saw me. They asked what was wrong, and I told them. I told them I had to take this medicine, and I was scared about what it might do to me. And then, for some reason, I opened up and told them about everything I'd been feeling. And those three girls, who I had barely gotten to know in my first two years at UA, said, "We're here for you."

We were supposed to be going to a recruitment event for the sorority that day. A mandatory event. Instead, they said, "It's okay. We're going to sit here with you. You're gonna take that medicine, and we'll watch out for you. It'll be fine."

I was shocked that they cared as much as they did.

The medication didn't have any negative effects. I *was* fine. And while the meds didn't fix everything for me, they definitely allowed me to care more. To invest in my life again. And once I cared again, my heart was set on fire for the Lord. Those sorority sisters kept me accountable. The four of us would become great friends after that. They watched out for me. We went to church together. We had all kinds of conversations, and it wasn't just about me. We talked about all of the struggles they were having, and we bonded over those. And then we just started having fun together.

It was so weird to me: going through the lowest lows of my life somehow led me back to the Lord and into the arms of these friendships.

For so long it had felt like even my family wouldn't accept me and my feelings, let alone any of my peers. So to have these girlfriends there for me was huge.

I started journaling on a regular basis to help me get through it all. I found it amazing just how much it helped to write down my feelings and thoughts, hopes and dreams.

I went back to church. I carried a notebook and pen into church with me every day. Brady came right along with me, at least as far as going to church. He never missed church on Sundays. There were Sundays when I went to church with him and his family. But it's almost like the better I got, and the more on fire I was for the Lord, the harder it was for Brady to keep up. We were both running this race for God, but he kept going at a comfortable pace while I began to sprint. He was at church every Sunday, but on Saturdays he was still going to parties and doing whatever.

If there's one thing I learned, it's that you can't pull somebody somewhere they don't wanna go.

We still had issues. I still felt like I couldn't trust him. I wondered about him sometimes. I didn't understand his behavior. As I said, I wouldn't learn about some of the things he was hiding from me until years later. It was just a feeling I had. I lived in fear that he was cheating on me or doing things at parties that would hurt me. Things I didn't know about.

I did my best to ignore that feeling. I loved him. He loved me. I wanted with all my heart to make it work.

But the first time I ever heard God speak to me, He told me to break up with Brady.

I was in church with one of my girlfriends when it happened. It wasn't a big booming voice like something you'd hear in a movie; it was more like an internal knowing. An internal whisper that wasn't mine. It wasn't *me* talking. I *wanted* to be with Brady. I wanted to make it work. I'd been in love with him for seven years!

I just couldn't deny what I'd heard. I heard God whisper, "You have to let go."

It wasn't a question. It was clarity. I knew it had to be done.

The night before it happened, Brady and I had gotten into an argument. We'd gotten into lots of them. At that point it was almost a cycle.

He showed up after church with flowers to apologize. He was so adorable and sweet—but I looked at him and said, "I don't want to do this. I can't do this anymore."

Of course he didn't believe me. He was sure I didn't mean it. "We've been together almost four years!" he said.

But I explained to him that I felt God speak to me, and it was time for this relationship to end. And it ended. And as soon as he left, I felt this overwhelming peace.

I knew I had done the right thing.

CHAPTER 12

Breakup Skinny

Brady proved me right: when we broke up, he immediately started hooking up with other girls. I knew he didn't love them, and it made me feel sick that the intimate moments we shared might not always have meant the same thing to him as they did to me.

At that point, the thought of allowing myself to have sex again, with anyone, became upsetting and hurtful to me.

I learned a lot from my relationship with Brady, including a lot of what not to do.

It doesn't matter how much you love somebody. If your relationship is not built on the right foundation, it's just going to end up hurting you more in the end. The fact that we started our relationship by sneaking around in secrecy was a lot of fun, but it wasn't a solid foundation. We started with him cheating on his girlfriend to be with me. So doesn't it make sense that he might turn out to be someone who wouldn't always be reliable in the way I wanted a man to be reliable?

I do think that the Lord can completely heal us. There are cases where something starts on a rocky foundation, but both people can grow and change and live happily ever after. If it's supposed to happen, it's going to happen. I believe that. I believe that the Lord can restore marriages and relationships of all kinds. But when we broke up, Brady went in the opposite direction.

I spent some time by myself, thinking about what I'd been through and what I wanted in the future. I wasn't interested in dating again right away. I didn't think my heart could take it. But I wrote down a long list of qualities I would like to see in a partner—a list that included trust, and honesty, and someone who wasn't interested in partying all the time, but who was up for an adventure, and who came from a good family and offered stability. I wanted to be with someone funny, someone who didn't make me question whether he'd chosen me, who had good friends, and for sure someone who was on the same sort of spiritual path I was on.

Three months later, I met Austin.

I had written down all these things that I wanted in a partner, and Austin fit a lot of them.

We started hanging out, but before we even kissed I knew it was too soon. I told Austin it was too soon. "I like you, I do, but I'm still in love with somebody else," I said.

Even though I had made the right decision about Brady, I still loved him, you know? Those feelings didn't fade away the instant I broke it off. I had been in love with the boy for seven years—that was one-third of my life!

"I don't care," Austin said. "I want to pursue you."

He was so sure of himself. There was no doubt. He wanted to pursue me, and only me. This wasn't a game to him. He "chose" me. Isn't that something every girl wants to hear? How could I say no?

So we started dating, and Austin taught me the way a girl should be treated. He was just so good to me, all the time, in every way.

I won't get into every detail of our relationship. I'll just say that Austin was exactly the kind of guy a girl ought to marry. He was trustworthy. Truly trustworthy. He was loving. He was kind. He was adventurous. We could talk forever. He made me belly-laugh like no one else could. He made me feel like the most important person in the room, no matter what room we were in. He came from a good family. He truly checked every box.

We dated for a year and a half, and I thought for sure this was it. Austin was never shy about wanting to marry me, and I honestly believed it would happen. He loved me, and I loved him. It was different from the way I loved Brady, but it was definitely love.

I kept telling myself, *I'll live on a farm in Alabama, and be a mom, and volunteer at our kids' school, and life will be good!*

That life sounded *so* good, actually. Contentment has always sounded like something that would be so nice to have. But a part of me thinks I was never supposed to have that life.

In college, I took a women's studies course. The course filled an elective requirement, and someone told me it was a good online class to take, so I was all about it. But I was shocked when it hit me in so many ways. Being from the South, I was raised with the idea that being a feminist is something terrible. My brother and his friends would make fun of me and call me a feminist, as if that word were a slur. But once I took that class and did more research and reading on my own, I realized that a feminist isn't somebody who "hates men."

It's someone who believes in the value and worth of women, and who wants women to have the same *rights* as men.

When somebody calls me a feminist now, I'm like, "I one thousand percent am!" Of course I want women to have the same rights!

People will argue that men and women are different, and that's fine. We all have different strengths. But women should not be oppressed in any way. And we *are*. We have been for a very long time.

After that women's studies course, I even looked more closely at what the Bible has to say about the roles of men and women, and I think a lot of people in our society have misinterpreted what the Bible says. Especially in the South.

The Bible talks about how men should honor women like the church, and women should be there to serve a man, but what seems to get lost is that men and women are supposed to be equally serving *each other*. It's not that the man is any more important than you are. If you're both serving each other, then both of your needs are going to be met equally.

That is not how it's been working, and I think that's why we see such a strong women's movement now, with more and more women taking leadership roles. It's gotten to the point where women have been shut down, and shut down, and shut down, and now we're like, "No!" It's in our nature to want to be equally a part of this world. And if men were serving us like the church, then we wouldn't have all these places where we aren't allowed, or where we make less money than men. If we were living equally, our careers wouldn't automatically take a back seat when children come into the picture, either. So many of the women I had seen in my life gave up their careers after having babies. Their lives changed completely as they became stay-at-home moms, or working moms who were still the first call for anything having to do with the kids. Meanwhile, their husbands' lives didn't really change too much. How is that fair?

If we were equal, I would not have been automatically thinking that I should go live wherever my husband lives. The assumption with Austin was that if we got married, we would live the simple life in Alabama. That wasn't only his assumption, it was mine! I barely even considered asking Austin to move somewhere else to back me up while I pursued my own dreams. And I was still trying to figure out what those dreams were. I studied communications, thinking I might go into public relations. But to take a job in PR, I would probably have to move to a big city, and I wasn't sure I wanted to do that. Austin worked as a contractor, and I had a serious knack for design and a love for beautiful homes. So I started thinking about a career in interior design. I had watched *Fixer Upper* on TV, and read *The Magnolia Story*, and I wanted to be the next Joanna Gaines. I even got a job at a high-end furnishings store just to learn a little bit more about the business. The hope was that I could find a career that could be pursued closer to home, a career that wouldn't require me to leave Austin behind.

Even though I didn't want to admit it at the time, I was doing it for a boy. But I think way deep down the idea of letting a husband take the lead as far as a career goes didn't sit right with me—in part because right near the beginning of my relationship with Austin, I got a taste of a very different life.

Because my parents worked in cosmetology with the Paul Mitchell company, and in the hopes of getting an internship for my communications/PR degree, I contacted someone in their corporate PR department in Los Angeles. I sent them a résumé and interviewed on the phone, and they hired me for a summer internship between my junior and senior years.

My dad dropped me off at a tiny studio apartment above a laundromat and a Mediterranean restaurant on Westwood Boulevard, bought me some groceries, and said goodbye. It was the first time I had ever lived on my own more than fifteen minutes from my parents' house. It was the first time I'd lived in a big city. And I *loved* it.

I was definitely a little scared at first, but I was super surprised how brave and willing I was to venture off alone in a new place.

I went to work every day in a beautiful office in Century City, and I hung out with people from work sometimes, but I spent most of my free time alone, just exploring the city. I walked Rodeo Drive in Beverly Hills. I went out to Santa Monica and dipped my toes in the Pacific Ocean. I went hiking. I missed Austin, and I talked to him on the phone a lot, but I was never all that lonely being so far from home. I'll admit there were times when I was walking around or looking at the sunset when I wished I had someone there to share it with me. But it was the first time I ever felt truly independent, and I *liked* that feeling.

My internship lasted only two months, and the job didn't entail much more than pulling product for gifting and clipping articles and mentions from magazines, but toward the end of it I was thinking, *Wow, I think I could live here. I could love this life. I love the energy. I love going to work. How much fun would it be to do this all the time?*

As soon as I got back to Alabama and back to UA, that new feeling sort of faded away. All of a sudden it seemed like so many of my friends were getting engaged—and I wasn't. I felt like I'd fallen behind somehow. I was the one who was supposed to get engaged before everybody else, I thought. I'd had a boyfriend from high school right into college!

That feeling of wanting to get engaged, of wanting to go back to "the norm," the things other girls around me were doing, definitely contributed to my belief that Austin and I were going to get engaged. He felt it too, and toward the end of our senior year, we made plans to go look at rings.

There was one big problem, though: I still had feelings for Brady.

I had talked to Brady off and on. We texted now and then. Our lives had been so entangled, it was hard not to. We had friends in common. We would run into each other around town occasionally. We would wind up being invited to mutual friends' weddings, so we had to stay cordial. I was up-front with Austin about all of it. I told him whenever we ran into each other, or he texted, and I even told him sometimes that I missed him for one reason or another. I didn't think I wanted to get back together with him. I just missed him.

But a week before we were going to go look at rings, Austin looked at me and said, "You still love him, don't you?"

I hesitated just long enough that he knew my answer before I said it.

Austin broke up with me right there. He had poured a year and a half into this relationship, and so had I. He was such a great guy, and I had deep feelings for him. But my old feelings for Brady just wouldn't go away.

After all the praying I'd done, I believed that the Lord was trying to tell me something.

Oh, my gosh, I thought. *I do still love him.* So I reached out.

I went to see him, fully convinced that he was the love of my life. Why else would I have these feelings? Why else would I let go of a guy who was so good to me in order to get back together with this boy I had fallen for at first sight, and who had caused me so much heartbreak?

Brady and I got together, and I told him, "I still love you. I haven't got over you. I just ended this relationship with a person that was great to me, because I haven't gotten over you."

I opened up and shared my whole heart with him. Brady told me he'd been on a date recently, but that he wasn't seeing anybody else. I took that as a good sign. I thought we'd both had a chance to mature a little bit. The timing felt right.

Brady told me it had been hard for him to see me in a serious relationship with somebody else for the last year and a half. He didn't understand how I was ready to be with somebody that seriously so quickly after our relationship ended. He asked me whether Austin and I had sex, and I told him that we had. Twice. Only twice in a year and a half. I mean, it wasn't like it was a casual thing. We loved each other. But still, I found myself apologizing to Brady about it. As if I had done something wrong.

Brady said he didn't like hearing it, but there also wasn't much he could do about it.

He said he still loved me.

We started kissing, and all of those late-night back-seat feelings came rushing back. We made out . . . and we hooked up. I wouldn't have done it if I didn't feel sure in that moment that we were getting back together. But just a few days later, he sort of mentioned that he'd been on more than "one date" with another girl. Then I found out that he was actually *dating* this other girl. They were *together*.

He had lied to me. Again.

I was so angry at him. "I just told you I love you," I said. "You said you love me, too!"

I felt used.

Then he said something that crushed me.

"I'll always love you and care for you," he said, "but, like, I don't see you as a wife anymore."

"What?" I said. "*Why?*"

He said it was because I'd had sex with another guy.

My chin just about hit the floor. I stared at him, thinking, *How dare you?*

Brady had gone off and had sex with other girls he did not love. Then he started dating this girl who was a quintessential good girl. I knew from mutual friends that she had never even been kissed, so of course she was a virgin, which made the whole thing worse for me, because *he's* the one who took my virginity. And now he was thinking I'm not wife material anymore because I had sex? Twice? With one other guy who I was in love with? A guy I thought I was gonna marry?

It was just about the most one-sided, misogynistic double standard I'd ever heard.

And it *killed* me.

I couldn't eat. I couldn't sleep. I just couldn't stop thinking about it. My stomach turned in knots, and I started losing a ton of weight from the anxiety and guilt and shame of the whole situation. Over and over I kept thinking, how had I messed this up so badly? I'd given up the best guy ever . . . for this?

Now I was stuck in the monotony of what living in Tuscaloosa had become for me, living with my parents, with no boyfriend, and not knowing what to do with my life.

"You need to get your mind off it," my mom told me. "You need to do something fun. Why don't you go for Miss Alabama again?"

"USA?"

"Yeah."

The thought of it surprised me. I did love being onstage. I loved performing. Even though I had stopped doing pageants and slipped into a period of depression, in part because of the pressures of the pageant world, I remembered those few minutes onstage as being some of my happiest moments ever. Maybe my mom was right.

"Mom, the pageant's in like two weeks. There's no way."

"If I call them and they say you can do it, will you do it?"

My mind was spinning. I was so sure they'd say no that I told my mom, "Sure."

Mom called back and told me that Paula, the pageant director, said I could do it. "But you have to fill out all the information *today*."

"Today?"

Normally I spent the whole year prepping for a big pageant like that. I would pay somebody to tell me what to write on my bio. How could I possibly do it *that day*? How could I possibly get ready in *two weeks*?

My friends were like, "Just do it. It doesn't matter. You look great . . . go!"

I did sort of miss the pageant world. I missed some of the people. I missed getting all dressed up and working so hard to achieve something. I definitely missed the feeling of being up onstage. But most of all, it felt like it would be the perfect distraction from everything I was feeling.

So I went for it.

I pulled up old Google docs of previous applications, put in what I thought still mattered, and sent it in. I had stopped dyeing my hair, so I couldn't use my old headshot. The only photo I had was more of a cool, edgy type shot that a guy took of me for his photography portfolio. It wasn't a typical glam shot at all. But it's all I had. So I sent it.

We went to a dress shop, tried on a dress, and bought it. We tailored some of the stuff in my closet, and that was all we had time to do. I caught up on some current events, and before I knew it, the two weeks was up.

There's nothing like being overwhelmed and busy to keep you from having to feel the pain of a breakup!

There's probably not anything less healthy, either.

Driving to Montgomery for the weekend pageant with my mom, I said, "What am I doing?"

We were laughing about how quickly we'd thrown it all together.

"I must enjoy losing," I said. "I guess I'm a first-place loser. We should get T-shirts made that say 'First-Place Loser!'"

My mom laughed. "Just go and have fun," she said.

We didn't tell anybody I was entering the pageant, so I didn't have my usual cheering section—but I also had none of the pressure.

As soon as we got there, everyone seemed to notice that I'd lost a ton of weight. I was at my lowest competition weight ever—and every single person I ran into told me how great I looked. "Wow, Hannah. You are stunning! How did you get so skinny?"

"Well, it wasn't on purpose. I broke up with my boyfri—"

"Ohhhh," they said. "Breakup skinny is the *best* kind of skinny. Good for you!"

I took their compliments as best I could, and I just ran with them. With no potato-chip-colored hair and no time to prepare, I got up on that stage and I gave it all I had to give. I didn't try to be anybody other than myself—and I made it to the Top 5.

Then they announced the second runner-up, and all that was left was two of us.

I stood onstage with the prior year's runner-up, and she grabbed hold of my hands and started saying a little prayer for us both, and I thought for sure she was going to win. The competition was hers to lose. And all of a sudden they announced the winner, and the audience started cheering, and I didn't even hear what they said.

"Hannah," the girl said, squeezing my hands and looking me in the eye. "It's *you*!"

"What?" I looked around, and I realized I'd won!

Instead of gracefully putting my hand over my heart or putting my hands over my mouth in the ladylike pose I'd practiced since I was a toddler, I raised my arms in victory and started jumping up and down like I'd just won a game of Uno at home with my family.

I could not believe it. After the last few years of trying so hard to look and act like somebody else, I walked in as myself, and I *won*.

I won by being me.

CHAPTER 13

WHAT YOU DON'T KNOW MIGHT HURT YOU

In the South, the pressure for girls to hurry up and get married is real.

Just one week after Austin and I broke up, an older lady at the store where I worked told me I should get on Match.com and start searching for a new boyfriend as soon as possible. "No time to waste!" she said.

I didn't know her, and she didn't know me, but she acted like she had every right to give me that advice just because she'd overheard me say something about being single.

The next day, at Walmart, I ran into my old PE coach from high school, and she asked, "Are you seeing anybody?"

"No ma'am," I said. "I'm actually not right now. I was dating somebody for a while, but we recently broke up."

"Well," she said, "as long as you find somebody and you're married and have kids in the next couple of years, you'll be fine!"

I thought she was kidding. She wasn't. She was dead serious.

At twenty-three, that was *not* what I wanted to hear.

In the grocery store, just one day later—I can hardly believe myself that this all happened in the same week—I ran in with my mom to grab something quick, and I was in my pajamas, and this old man in line started talking to my mom, and he looked at me and huffed and said: "You'll never get a husband dressed like that!"

I was like, "What the crap?"

I looked right back at him and said, "Well, good thing I'm here looking for supper, and not a husband."

I still wasn't over the shock of losing Austin and Brady back-to-back. I had zero interest in finding somebody new. Even after coming home from Montgomery with the crown on my head and a sash across my chest, after being named the most beautiful girl in all of Alabama—which by some people's definition put me in the position of being one of the most eligible young women in the whole state that year—I still wasn't anywhere close to wanting to put myself out there again.

Actually, one of the things I was really excited about was that I would have a whole year just to focus on me.

During my reign I would have all kinds of duties, from community service projects to parades to speaking engagements at schools. The pageant duties would keep me busy straight through May 2018 as I built my experience and my résumé on the road to the nationally televised Miss USA pageant.

I got so excited just thinking about it. I was on my way to making a lifelong dream come true. So what if it wasn't the exact dream I'd had, of becoming Miss America? Being on this road meant every sacrifice I'd made was worth it. I was *going* to be Miss USA. I was sure of it. It was what God wanted for me. Why else would I have won the way I did?

*

Taking a year or so without dating anyone new was one of the best things I'd ever done for myself. From Tucker, to Brady, to my summer fling with Luke, to Brady again, and then Austin, and then my very short-lived attempt to go back to Brady, I hadn't gone more than three months without having a boy in my life since I was seventeen years old.

I started questioning why I'd done that, and why I wanted to get married right after college anyway. Having time to really see the world, whether it's through your career or your relationships, just getting outside of your own little bubble—I think it's important. And I think there's more time to do that than people think. You don't have to rush into everything. Why do we feel like we have to get all the degrees, get the wife, the husband, the kids, right away? I think if I had done that, I might have reached twenty-five and thought, *Oh, God, is this the rest of my life?*

I've been thinking about that a lot lately—the things I *thought* I wanted versus the way things turned out. If I had married Austin or Brady, my life would have been set in stone pretty quickly. And some people love that feeling. But I really don't think that would have been right for me. I mean, none of the things that have happened since then would have happened. None of them!

I feel like every day now is a new *something*, and I am so thankful that my plans way back when didn't work out. The more I see the world, the more excited I am at the possibilities opening up—for my life, my career, all of it! One of the things I've learned these last few years is just how young I really am. And I have to stop myself every once in a while and remind myself of that. "You're still in your twenties, Hannah. And you know what? You're doing okay, kid. You'll figure it out."

This messy stuff is all just a part of it. And God bless this mess—because without the messes, without all the screwups, without some of the ups and downs, how would we ever learn to do things better? To do things the way we want to do them, for *ourselves*?

After the breakup with Austin and the ending with Brady, I participated in my church's 21 Days of Prayer, where we went to church every day at 6:00 a.m. for twenty-one days straight, just to get into the habit of praying every morning and making it part of a routine. I journaled through that. I journaled that whole year.

Journaling gave me time to think, and one of the things I thought about was what I had learned from my two longest relationships, and what each of them taught me about what I really wanted in a husband.

I made lists one day of what Austin taught me, and what Brady taught me, and guess what? Neither of them, individually, had all the qualities I wanted and needed in order to be happy. But between them, they each offered so much that I loved.

From Austin, I learned that I wanted to be in a relationship where I could talk about our faith and mention Jesus in everyday conversations, naturally, and often. Austin was so sure of his faith that I didn't need to think about it. It came easy to us. It came naturally for him.

Austin was fun, and silly, which meant we laughed together. He was a hard worker. He was a man's man. He was great with kids, and he was great with me. He would clean my car sometimes without me asking. He would make me breakfast. He would do the things that I don't necessarily love doing, which made life easier for me, but he was also someone who wouldn't always put up with my crap. If I was being needy or selfish in some way, he would call me on it, and yet do it in a way that didn't hurt me. He was also very accepting of the fact that he wasn't perfect, either, which again just made our relationship feel natural. I loved all of that.

But with Brady, I had this *passionate* love. We knew each other physically so well, and I want that in the future for sure. Passion is a big thing for me, and not just in the bedroom or the back seat of a pickup truck. I love having passionate conversations. I liked to go fishing with Brady just because he loved fishing so much and would get so excited when he talked about it. On the other hand, Brady wouldn't dance with me, even when we went out to our favorite bar. I want a guy who'll dance with me! Is that too much for a girl to ask?

I want someone who's intelligent, and who's going to be successful. They both had that going for them. But I want to be successful, too, and I want a man who isn't afraid to let me be the star of the show. Austin and I were both stars, and it felt like everything was a competition at times. Brady was much more willing to just sit back and clap for me. Even when I went to LA for my internship, we talked, and he said, "It is so cool to see you being independent and taking charge of your life."

I wanted a husband—someday—who could be all of those things.

But I still wasn't ready to look for him. I had a pageant to win. And I don't know if it was the stress of that, or if something was up with my hormones, or what, but in the months leading up to Miss USA, I developed the worst acne of my life.

My skin actually hurt, like I was wearing a mask that was on too tight.

I caked on makeup to try to cover it up, and of course that only made the acne worse. People in the pageant world kept saying, "What are we going to do about your skin?"

It hurt my self-confidence so bad, I actually canceled some of my public appearances. And that made me feel even worse. I had sponsors spending money to support me, and I felt like I was letting them down, even though it wasn't my fault. I tried a bunch of different medications and treatments, and none of it worked.

My body was stressed out, and what I'm kind of realizing now is that I might have been dealing with a little bit of anorexia. I didn't know it at the time, but I feel like a lot of people who have had eating disorders sometimes don't know it until they're out of it, sometimes for years.

It started with the breakups, being so heartbroken that I physically couldn't eat. But then I continued the not-eating habit straight through the Miss Alabama USA pageant, and for quite a while afterward. I was so stressed and kept myself so busy that I would think about eating, but then think, "Oh, I don't *have* to eat. You survived the post-breakup not eating just fine!" I convinced myself that it was okay to eat nothing but one protein bar per day. I mean, today I can see that was clearly a problem. At the time, I thought it wasn't. But a lone protein bar a day is not enough.

I justified it because when I ate like that, I dropped weight fast, and I didn't have to work out that much. Then people started praising me about my body because I am naturally athletic. When I drop weight, I look thin, but still strong. So it looked like I was working out when I was quietly thinking, *Oh, so all I have to do is not eat, and people think I look good.*

Because my acne was so out of my control, I put all my effort into trying to control my body. I would get so skinny that you could see my natural muscles, whether or not those muscles were strong. No one knew how stressed I was. No one knew how depleted I was. At the expense of my own health, I finally got the thigh gap I always wanted.

I worked with a trainer for the final few days before the Miss

Alabama USA pageant, and I ended up having to gain weight. For a beauty pageant.

"You're so skinny right now," my trainer said, "we need to add back a little bit of curve on you."

I just couldn't seem to please everyone, no matter what I did. I could not make my body look like some other person's, and when I did, it's because I was having health issues. I was underweight.

I sit at about 145 pounds when I'm healthy, and at one point I was 118. I dropped from a size 4-6 to a size 00.

There were times during this period when I had friends ask if I was okay because I was so skinny. I looked sick to them. Yet in the pageant world, that's exactly when people would tell me I looked good.

There's one picture of me where my face is so thin you can see a vein in my face, and I used to think that was one of my best looks! I see that picture differently now.

Before I knew it, the big Miss USA pageant was right around the corner—and my face looked awful because of the acne. My confidence was shot.

Right before the big weekend, I prayed: "Okay, God. This is it. How could it *not* be? You've led me this far. I'm supposed to be Miss USA . . . aren't I?"

I guess God's answer was "No," because I didn't even place.

I was so confused. I couldn't understand: Why would God give me this amazing opportunity, but then put this barrier in my way? I was always told I had a pretty face, and my body needed work. Now my body looked right for the competition, but my face was a mess.

The acne did me in. When all was said and done, Miss USA was still a beauty pageant, and caked-on makeup over zits just wasn't gonna win it. I finally thought a part of me was fixed, and then this other thing happened.

I honestly dealt with the loss okay. I was already so down about my acne that not placing in the competition didn't make me feel much worse. I felt like nobody was looking at me, anyway. They were just looking at my acne. So in a way I was glad when it was all over.

✳

A month later, I went out with a couple of friends of mine, and over lunch they asked me what I was gonna do next.

I really had no idea.

They asked me if I was seeing anyone, and I laughed. I'd had no time.

"Plus, how am I ever gonna meet someone now?" I said. "I don't know how to meet anyone outside of school."

"You should go on *The Bachelor*!" one of them said.

I laughed. "Maybe," I responded. "At this point it might be my only option."

I wasn't serious. I had barely even watched the show. I had only seen a few episodes, ever. But it's so weird that it came up that day, because that same afternoon I got a call from a phone number I didn't recognize. I recognized that it was an LA area code, though, so I picked up. I thought maybe it was somebody I'd known from my Paul Mitchell days, or something.

It wasn't.

It was a producer from *The Bachelor*, saying that someone had nominated me, anonymously, and they wanted to know if I was interested in auditioning for the next season of the show.

"Is this some kind of a joke?" I asked.

"No," they said. "We really liked the application they sent in, and we love that you were Miss Alabama. We're interested in seeing more. Can you send us a video, just telling us a little more about yourself?

It doesn't have to be anything formal or professional, but we'd need you to send us something in the next forty-eight hours."

"I . . . um . . . sure!" I said.

They gave me all the info I needed, and I immediately called my friends from lunch.

"Did *you* do this?" I asked.

They insisted it wasn't them. They were as shocked as I was. I called my mom, and it wasn't her. I had absolutely no idea who submitted my name to the show.

I shot a little audition tape on my phone, and then I went and rented the most recent season of *The Bachelor*, starring a guy named Arie, just so I could see what I was getting myself into. I sat on the sofa and took notes on it. I counted the number of outfits the girls wore, and it was a lot! I wasn't sure I could afford to buy that many outfits. I took note of what happened each week, and what happened on the group dates and the solo dates. I loved that they were traveling around the world and seeing such beautiful places. *I* wanted to travel the world and see beautiful places! What's the worst that could happen?

At the same time, I also started watching the latest season of *The Bachelorette*, which had just started airing that May—and after seeing that show, I wasn't sure I wanted to do it. I looked at all of these guys they'd cast in *The Bachelorette*, and only one of them seemed like somebody I might like to date. It was a guy named Colton Underwood, a twenty-six-year-old who talked openly about how he was choosing to remain a virgin until marriage. I respected that about him. Not only that, but he was super cute, and he played football, and he'd started a charitable foundation, and he just seemed like the nicest guy.

I actually told some of my friends, "The only way I'll do this show is if they choose Colton as the next Bachelor."

In the meantime the producers watched my cell-phone video, and they invited me to come to Atlanta for an in-person interview. Atlanta was one of the last locations for casting calls around the country. The show selected everybody by the end of August, they said, so there wasn't much time.

I still had the acne issue, and I didn't think I wanted to do it, so I really didn't take it that seriously. But my mom said, "Just go! Give it a try. It'll be fun!"

So I went.

On the way to Atlanta, I got a text from a videographer I had hired to shoot some footage for me just before the Miss USA pageant. She was a friend of a friend, and I didn't know her very well, but she texted me a "Hey girl!" and told me that *she* was the one who had sent in the anonymous application!

I called her from the car. "Why?" I asked.

"I woke up in the middle of the night," she said, "and felt like I should nominate you for *The Bachelor*. I don't know why. I hope you don't mind."

"Well, they called me! I am on my way to an audition right now," I said.

"I *knew* it," she said. She was so excited for me. "And now I've just been watching the show, and I love Colton."

"I've started to watch it too, and the only guy that I want to date is Colton."

"Right?" she said. "I just thought y'all were so much alike. And I don't know. I have a feeling. I really think it's going to be Colton."

Colton Underwood was *not* the person most people assumed would be the next Bachelor. I was quickly discovering all sorts of social media that followed the series obsessively, and he just wasn't the

150

number one choice of most fans. So it was kind of amazing that this woman was thinking the same thing I was thinking.

"I want it to be him so bad," I told her. "I can't see myself with anybody else."

It was also kind of amazing to me that she had filled out an application for me. I mean, we only had one conversation about the break-ups I'd been through. We talked about it one day when we were riding together in the car to get to a beach to shoot some video. That was it.

I started to wonder if maybe this whole thing was meant to be. Like maybe this wasn't something random.

In Atlanta, I had *fun*, just like my mom wanted me to—mostly because I had no expectations about what might happen. They put me in a room with some of people who worked on the show, and they turned a camera on, and they asked me all about *me*. I was so used to answering questions in front of a microphone that I just put on my Pageant Patty smile and answered whatever they asked. It was easy.

My childhood best friend, Olivia, also happened to be in Atlanta, so I got a chance to see her that trip as well. It really felt like everything made sense. As if maybe this was about taking a path I never would have chosen for myself, but which definitely felt like the right path.

Apparently the producers liked the answers I gave in Atlanta, 'cause after I got back to Alabama they called again, and they asked me if I could come to the final round of auditions in LA.

"I don't know if I can afford to fly out there," I said. I didn't have any money. I had just spent a fortune on the dress and preparation for Miss USA.

"Oh, no," they said. "We'll fly you out."

How could I say no to a free trip to LA?

I flew out, they put me up in a nice hotel, and soon I walked into a conference room with a bunch of producers who ran the show.

"Just so you know," I told them, "I'm not doing this unless it's Colton."

They laughed, but I was dead serious. I think my attitude surprised them. I clearly wasn't desperate to be on their show. I didn't care one way or the other, and I think that worked in my favor. I wasn't faking anything. I wasn't super nervous. I wasn't trying too hard.

I was just *me*.

They turned a camera on, and they asked me questions, and I smiled and started listing off my accomplishments, including what I'd been up to in my year as Miss Alabama USA. But they stopped me. They started asking deeper questions, about my family and how I grew up.

Honestly, I had never been asked those kinds of questions in my whole life. As I think I already mentioned, my parents didn't believe in therapy. So I'd never had anybody other than a close friend ask me questions about my personal life, or my emotions, or the guys I'd dated, and I'd certainly never had anyone try to dig down into my personality traits to see how I might react to different situations. It felt good to me that somebody was listening and wanted to see me.

I was just talking all sweet and stuff when one of the casting people asked whether I ever had road rage. I didn't really want to admit that I did, so I started to talk about how I never cussed. My parents cussed, but at that point I had trained myself to say "frick" or "fridge" instead of the F-word, and "shizz" or "shat" instead of the S-word.

But the more I kept talking, the more I realized that I do get road rage. Sometimes I full-out scream in my car, and sometimes I cuss when I scream.

Before I knew it, I was opening up and admitting to myself that I held this little tank of rage in a spot beside my stomach.

No, I kept thinking. *I'm full of joy!* But this interview felt like what I imagined therapy would feel like; like I'd cracked and opened up a feeling I didn't want to acknowledge. I thought those casting folks were looking for the perfect girl, the pageant girl, and such a big part of me is definitely that, and definitely filled with joy. But if you've read this far, you know that's not my full story.

I couldn't believe how much I was opening up, and to *strangers*. I liked it. And it kind of made me wonder if going on *The Bachelor* would help me do that more.

I was open and honest with them. I was "real" with them. And two weeks later they called and told me they were prepared to offer me a spot on the show.

I asked them if Colton was going to be the Bachelor, and they said they couldn't tell me, but it was implied that I was gonna be happy if I said "Yes."

They gave me a few hours to think about it, and one of the first things I did was reach out to Brady.

I know, I *know*. But I still had feelings for him. I wanted to let him know I had an opportunity to go on a TV dating show. I wanted to see if he would stop me. A big part of me was *hoping* he would stop me. Even after everything that had happened, I wanted him to fight for me . . . because if he did, then maybe it could still be *us*.

But he didn't. He didn't even try. And that was pretty much the last straw for me. So I finally let it go. Of all things, deciding to go on *The Bachelor* was what finally helped me get over him. *Praise the Lord!*

I said "Yes!"

As the world would find out that September, the producers did choose Colton to be the next Bachelor. I found out for sure it was Colton just before we started shooting the show in LA.

It felt like fate. I could hardly believe it. It felt like everything was falling into place in a way that I couldn't have arranged if I'd tried. I kept praying about it, asking, "Is this really how you want me to find a husband? I mean, why else is this all falling into place the way it is?"

I didn't hear God's voice like I did in church nearly three years earlier. But everything in my heart said "Yes!"

So I signed on the dotted line, and I scrambled to get myself ready.

The show didn't provide wardrobe for the women, just for the "leads" on the shows. And I didn't get paid anything to go compete for Colton's affections for all those weeks, either. So Sherri Hill, who designed my dress for Miss USA, let me take some prom dresses from her collection to wear for the rose ceremonies. We tailored some of my old Miss Alabama USA dresses, too, and I packed up some other clothes from my closet. There are girls who spend thousands of dollars on dresses before going on these shows. But I couldn't do that.

When I left for LA, I had $70 in my bank account.

It was a total leap of faith for me to take that trip. It all happened so fast, I didn't really think about what the consequences might be.

Taking a leap of faith and doing something spontaneous in life can be really fun. But you have to ask yourself: *Is this leap going to be worth the potential fall?*

Maybe that's something I should have spent a *little* more time thinking about before I put myself on national television.

CHAPTER 14
Welcome to Bachelor Nation

Moving into the Bachelor mansion in Agoura Hills outside Los Angeles was not unlike moving into the dorms for the Miss Alabama pageants. Only the girls here weren't competing for a crown. They were competing for a husband.

Just like in the pageant world, I could see that everybody was comparing themselves to everybody else. We were checking out the outfits we'd brought, and the evening gowns we'd brought, and the fancy shoes everybody had. And when girls are put in tight quarters in a competitive environment, it sure is easy for all of that surface stuff to get into your head.

After everything I had been through, I wasn't interested in any of the drama—and, ironically, that caused me a lot of drama. I chose to stay in my room reading or writing in my journal when other girls were socializing, which made some of them think I was kind of standoffish. I went on camera without wearing makeup, which made some of the girls think I must be nuts, but it was only because I was trying to get my face to clear up.

This wasn't a competition for me. I really thought being put on this show was a new path for me to find a husband. I mean, why wouldn't it be? Stranger things than this had happened in my life. So I took it seriously. I was there to get to know Colton. Not to make friends, not to make enemies, and not to make a career for myself on TV.

Also? I had nothing to lose. Truly, nothing.

As a result, I apparently did a lot of things people don't usually do in front of the cameras. I was there to have fun, so I had fun. I made the crew laugh. I was silly. I goofed around. Just being me and letting loose a little bit caught the attention of the cameramen, and people on the crew kept saying, "That was great!"

I was the first one to eat a bug on camera, because why not? If they were going to challenge us, I wasn't gonna let anybody show me up. I wanted to prove to Colton that I was up for any adventure. I had never been out of the country, and the first flight they put us on was a flight to Singapore—which I think is the longest flight you can take from the US. And I loved it!

It was like I'd won the lottery or something, getting to do all these adventurous things.

It felt like my whole life had changed, literally overnight.

In my one-on-one interviews in front of the cameras, I opened up my heart like a busted old river dam. It was like therapy to me. I shared stories from my past, and talked about my faith, and at one point I even told them about the murder of my aunt and cousins. Not all of it aired, and it wasn't up to me which parts aired and which didn't, but as you know if you watched the show, nothing about that part of my family history aired on TV.

Once again, it seemed to me as if that story was just too much for people to hear.

Once again, I put my story away. I hid it. I stuffed it all back down inside of me. But the feeling of that trauma was like lava down deep in a volcano, and it was starting to bubble. Those feelings needed to get out. And they would.

Rejection, fear, heartbreak—all of these emotions that I kept stuffing down inside me—would need to get unpacked eventually. And the thing I've learned since is that you either unpack them yourself, or the baggage is going to explode into every relationship and every experience you have. I know now how unhealthy this was for me, both emotionally and physically.

It scared me to think how much of my baggage had already exploded into every corner of my life, from past boyfriends, to my decision-making, to my fears, to friendships, to my relationship with God.

But maybe it's a good thing that it never aired. A camera is not a therapist. Neither is a social-media account. Pouring your heart out on TV or on social isn't necessarily going to help anyone feel better about themselves. In reality, I should have thought a lot more about what I did and said in a public setting. I should have thought of going on camera like somebody had read me my Miranda rights, like the detectives do on *Law & Order*: "Anything you say can and will be used against you in a court of law." Only the court in this case was the court of public opinion, and anything I said or did could be used against me in ways I couldn't even imagine at that time.

Caught up in the moment and enjoying the fun of it all, I didn't stop to think about what might happen later. I just rolled with it.

I was there to meet Colton, and when I did, I thought he was just as good-looking as when I'd seen him on TV. But almost immediately

I observed that he seemed a lot different when the cameras weren't rolling. He just seemed more uptight, or something. Something was just *off*. But I figured, hey, it's a television show, maybe it would just take some time to get to know each other. And he was everything I wanted on paper, so I wanted to give him that chance. Give *myself* that chance.

It was weird, though, after seeing Colton on a television show, to be showing up with certain assumptions and feelings about him, and then all of a sudden stepping out of a limousine, onto wet pavement, in front of a mansion, saying hi to him, and then walking into a mansion with all these other girls who were vying for his attention—it felt surreal. Was there that initial spark? Not like I'd expected, honestly, but I figured, *Give it time.*

When I finally got to sit down with Colton on that first night, they filmed us talking together, and they photographed us talking together, but they never showed that conversation on TV when the show aired. (If you want to know all the details of what happened on air, I encourage you to go rent Colton's season. It's definitely some good TV!)

I asked if he would pinkie-promise me something, and he said, "Sure." We locked our pinkies together, and I said, "We're gonna have an honesty policy. Like, if you're having concerns or you're questioning something, will you just tell me? Because I promise to always be honest with you, and I just want you to promise to always be honest with me."

"*Absolutely*," he said.

"If at any point you're not feeling it, please just let me know, and I'll do the same," I reiterated.

"I will," he said, as he looked me in the eyes and flashed that charming smile of his.

After all the thinking and list making I'd done about what I wanted in a future husband, honesty was absolutely my number one. I just wanted to be able to trust somebody, and everything I'd seen about Colton—his faith, his values—made me feel confident he could be that person.

I'm honest. *I'm* trustworthy. I don't think that's too much to ask for in a partner.

I don't think it's too much for any of us to ask for in a partner. I think we all need honesty in our relationships.

Clearly, when I didn't have it in the past, it had hurt me. And I didn't want to get hurt anymore.

Of all the guys on the previous season of *The Bachelorette*, Colton definitely seemed like the most faithful. I mean, he was a virgin. He was a virgin because of his faith, right? That meant, to me, that his faith was important to him. He'd been true to himself. That says a lot about a person, I thought. And after getting so badly burned by Brady, I was super attracted to someone whose morals and lifestyle seemed more aligned with mine.

Every time we sat down from that day on, I checked in with Colton. The first thing I asked him was, "Are we good? You okay? How *are* you?" And every time he smiled and said, "Yeah. I'm good. *We're* good."

What's obvious to anyone who watches the show is that the time contestants spend with the lead is actually super limited. It seems as if every exit speech contains some variation of the phrase, "I wish we had had more time together." That was definitely true for Colton and me, as it was for Colton and every one of the girls who got a rose and stuck around from week to week. He would be off on group dates, or on one-on-one dates, and there were times when there was all this stuff happening with other girls, and we didn't know about any of it. Some of us would learn things only after they aired the following

January! It's kind of crazy trying to get to know someone and trust someone with such a small amount of time together, but everyone kept telling me, "Trust the process. It works!"

So I did. I trusted the process. I trusted myself. I trusted that God wouldn't have led me down this road if I wasn't supposed to be there.

The Colton I did see, and the one I heard about from some of the other girls when they came back from their dates with him, wasn't exactly the same guy I'd seen on TV. In some ways, he didn't line up with all the characteristics I was looking for in a husband. There were times I wanted to leave. I'd think, *I don't know if Colton is right for me.* But everyone kept telling me to see it through, and I *wanted* to see it through. *If it's gonna happen, it's gonna happen,* I just kept thinking. That's just the way God's will works.

The idea of getting engaged to Colton wasn't about winning for me, despite what some fans and some of the other girls thought. It was just this I-wanna-know-if-this-could-work feeling. It was the purest thing. It truly was never about being the best on the show. I mean, I'm an achiever, but it wasn't that: I wanted love. I wanted it so bad I would have done anything to get someone to really love me in the way I wanted to be loved.

On our first date, I wasn't ready to open up. I went into the first night feeling very rehearsed and ready, as if it were a pageant. But we went on our first one-on-one date the very next day. I had only been there two days. I had barely ever watched the show. I didn't know what to expect, or what to do.

There were GoPro cameras mounted in the car. I was nervous. I wasn't ready for this. If this was really the guy I was going to be with, I wanted to be myself with him—and in front of all those cameras, I didn't feel ready to be myself with anyone.

Who are you going to be, Hannah? I was thinking. *Are you going to be your full self? Or the cookie-cutter version that probably got you this one-on-one in the first place?*

So far I had turned into Pageant Patty in front of the cameras—putting on the smile, saying the right things—and I didn't know how to get out of it. I felt stuck. How could I be myself with cameras up my nostrils?

When the first date aired, people made fun of me, saying it was the most cringeworthy date they had ever seen. And what they were really cringing at was me trying to figure out how to be *me*. They handed us glasses of champagne to make a toast, in the middle of the desert, in a jacuzzi, with a guy I'd only talked to twice since I'd arrived.

It wasn't as cringeworthy in real life as it looked on TV, but it was pretty cringeworthy.

Actually, that was an important moment for me. In that hot tub I realized that the polished, put-together, say-the-right-thing Pageant Patty me wasn't going to work on this show, and it wasn't what I wanted to give to this potential relationship. I decided to try to let my walls down, and to do that, I had to feel the awkward in between. And as I made that shift, I was basically a little doe in the headlights of the cameras.

There was all kinds of drama in the house with the other girls, and they aired a lot of that on TV. It honestly didn't make me look very good. I didn't have my phone when we were filming, but once I was home and started watching the show, I made the mistake of going on social media and getting a very harsh introduction to what it's like to be on the receiving end of haters in Bachelor Nation. A lot of people out there absolutely *hated* me based on what they saw on TV. These perfect strangers were calling me names that I will not repeat in public. I got hundreds of DMs saying the most horrible things about me. I even got a couple of death threats.

All of it made me feel terrible. I wasn't a celebrity. I'd never been on TV before. I had no training in this. I didn't have a manager or a publicist. I had no idea how to turn that noise off or filter it out. Every single comment and message hurt me personally.

But when we were filming, I didn't think about how things might look on TV, or look to other people. I kept my focus on Colton.

Still, I kept getting the feeling that something was off. A feeling like he didn't even want to be kissing me, you know? Some of the other girls felt like something was off, too, and honestly I didn't know what to think. Was he interested in me at all? We even had one conversation when I told him straight up (just like we'd promised to do for each other) that I was having doubts. After all the drama in the house, and as things were progressing while we had so little actual time together, I gave him this analogy: "I feel like I'm on this cliff. And with all the drama that's happened, I feel like I want to back away from the edge. Either that or I just want to jump, and really allow myself to start giving my heart to you."

And Colton looked at me and said, "Hannah, jump. I've already jumped. Jump with me."

It was so reassuring to hear him say that. I decided to try and put my fears away.

Still, the next time I had a chance to talk with him, it seemed to me like he still had some doubts about the two of us. So I asked him, "Do you remember what you said? Like, are we on the same page?" And once again, he answered, "Yeah."

So eventually, I started to allow myself to have feelings for him.

I would have never opened my heart to him at all if he hadn't said those things to me. *Okay*, I told myself. *He's honest. He's somebody I can trust.*

That's why I told Colton that I was falling for him. I opened up my heart and my mouth and let him know how much I liked him. It was a risky thing to do. It may have been too soon. I was serious about being there. I wanted it to work so bad. Maybe I was trying to push myself to feel more than I was feeling.

But the night after I said it, he gave me a rose—and I absolutely took that as an affirmation that he was falling for me, too.

Oh, God, I thought, feeling really hopeful about it. *We're on the same page!*

Finally.

✳

One thing I wanted to talk about with Colton, more than anything else, was his faith. Other than saying he was a virgin, he didn't reveal very much about his faith on TV. Religion and spirituality didn't seem to be something *anyone* talked about on *The Bachelor*. But I needed to know where he stood.

As far as I was concerned, we couldn't have a real relationship if we weren't aligned on faith. Being able to talk about Jesus was up at the top of my list of potential husband-material traits. But I'm not sure if many of the people working on that TV show understood. It was the first time in my life I was ever surrounded by so many people who didn't go to church, and some of them openly told me that they didn't believe in God. And that was okay with me. I found it really interesting talking to people with different perspectives than mine. But still, "my family, my friends back home in Alabama, that's the first thing they're gonna ask him," I said. "And if I haven't had this conversation with him, I can't bring him home."

When Colton asked me, on my second one-on-one date, to go to meet his family—which, if you aren't familiar with how things work on *The Bachelor*, was a really big deal—I thought, *Oh, wow.*

He had given me a rose, week after week. We were getting toward the end of filming. I thought for sure this meant that he was serious about me, and felt good about me, because he'd promised he would be honest with me. He said we were "good" every time I asked him. Getting invited on that date made me think for sure that I was gonna be in the top four, which would lead us to hometowns, where he would come to Alabama and meet my family. And I was so serious about it, my heart started racing. I kept thinking about the time we had spent together, and what it felt like when we kissed, and what it would be like for the two of us to be together outside of the show.

I had kissed only four boys in my life before I kissed Colton. This wasn't something I took lightly. I was there for marriage, and I kept thinking, *Am I ready for this?*

I was certain he was thinking *he* was ready for it, because that's what he told me week after week. That *he* was ready. That we could take this leap *together*.

But as soon as I got in the car to go on that date, I got this feeling in my gut that something was wrong. I didn't know what it was, but something just felt off. It's like we just weren't connecting the way we were supposed to. We were two very different people. Had I been fooling myself?

I should have listened to that feeling.

But I didn't. I kept thinking that being loved by this guy who was perfect for me on paper would be the right thing to happen. It would solve all of those insecurities. He *seemed* like the right person to love.

Instead, I tried to open up and connect with him on a deeper lever than I already had.

I sat down to dinner in a pretty pink Rachel Zoe dress that the show provided, and I said to Colton, "There's something that I've been wanting to ask you: I need to know if you're a man of God and what your relationship with Jesus is like before I take you home."

Colton didn't seem taken aback by my question. He talked to me about it. He was open and honest about it, and I suddenly felt so much better. My worry and fears went away. "You know," I said with a great big smile, "I feel so much more confident taking you home now."

In that moment, it felt like the floodgates of a loving relationship opened between us. It was as if talking about faith just released his heart, and he went into this monologue filled with some of the nicest things anybody's ever said to me.

And then he paused, and his whole demeanor changed, and he said, "But I can't get to where you are."

"Wait, *what?*" I said.

All of a sudden, after saying all these things about how special I was, he started talking about all the reasons it wasn't going to work between us.

I thought for a quick minute that maybe he had misunderstood the whole idea of "where I was," so I tried to make it clear: "I'm not *in love with you*, but, like, I am falling for you," I said. And he looked really uncomfortable when I said it.

"Yeah, I just . . ."

He started trying to explain himself, and it felt so awkward that I stopped him.

"Whoa," I said. "I thought we were on the same page, or I would never have said that. I would never have allowed myself to say it if I didn't feel like you were there with me."

I had set my bar of honesty high from the start, and apparently he had ducked right under it. In a matter of minutes, he busted all of my trust issues wide open—and I was *mad*.

He broke up with me, and I was like, "You know, I am glad you told me now."

In a way, I really *was* glad he did it. I would much rather know early on that someone's been withholding their true feelings than to find out after we got engaged.

But when Colton put me in the limo to send me home, all of the hurt and rejection I had ever felt came rushing up from inside of me. I thought about Brady, and how much he'd said he loved me, and yet somehow I wasn't enough for him. I thought about the pageants, and how many times I'd been told I had something "special," but that my "special" wasn't enough to win. I hated the feeling of not being enough for this guy. Or *any* guy. And I just went off about it.

"I'm f'in' pissed," I said. "I don't think his actions and his words really add up."

And I broke down in tears while holding my head high.

"It's just really frustrating," I said. "The desire in my heart is to be loved so fearlessly by somebody. I will not allow myself to not feel chosen every single day—and I'll wait till whenever that is."

When the breakup episode aired on TV, I think it was the first time anyone in Bachelor Nation started to take me seriously. I spoke so clearly and so articulately about what had happened and what I was feeling, there were people on social media who thought I must have been reading from a script. But that wasn't the case at all. I just spoke from my heart—my scarred, dented, bruised-up heart.

What people didn't know about me then were the things I've

shared with you in this book. The audience didn't know about the double breaking of trust that I'd suffered less than a year before I went on *The Bachelor*. It probably seemed silly to some people that I was so mad and upset about losing a guy I'd just met on a TV show. But the violation of trust that I experienced from Colton, a man who had specifically *promised* to be honest with me, opened up some old scars.

For other people, my little monologue in the limo turned into a feminist manifesto. It was wild. Clips of my limo-ride exit went viral, and all of a sudden people on social media, and in old-fashioned media, too, were calling me a good example of a modern feminist. They kept talking about how important it was for women to stand up for themselves the way I'd stood up for myself on the show.

Overnight I went from being a reality-TV pariah to becoming a public figure revered for my strength as a woman.

I can't even begin to tell you how good it felt to be received so positively by so many people, and to feel connected with so many people. As if all of these other women *got me*; as if I'd said what so many women should—but don't always—say when our love is treated carelessly.

Looking back, I'm just so proud of how I had come into my own during that season. I was so much more certain of what I wanted at that point than I'd ever been in my life. I was so plugged-in after all the journaling and reflection I'd done, and how free I'd felt to just be me on that show, that the truth came pouring out of me through all of the pain and the hurt.

A couple of years later, when I saw Colton come out as gay on *Good Morning America*, I'd see that same freeness for him—and it made me happy. (It also helped me to better understand why things just felt a little off between us—because he felt off with himself. He wasn't living the truth.) I didn't understand yet—not *deeply*, yet—what it meant to live the most private parts of your life on a television show. To feel like you couldn't be 100 percent who you are.

If I'd had some time to take it all in, to really live with it after the show ended, who knows where I would be today? But I didn't have time to do that—because next thing I knew, the producers were calling me, asking if I would like to audition to be the next Bachelorette.

CHAPTER 15

Skrrrrrip!

I was sitting in a hotel room, eating a cheeseburger with a chocolate *and* a vanilla milkshake, alternately crying and trying to repack all of my things, when some people from the show expressed interest in making me the next Bachelorette.

It had only been a few hours since Colton broke up with me.

"Eff you, guys!" I said. (Actually, I used the real F-word.) "There's no way. I'm hurt. And you're already talking to me about this?"

I went home feeling butt-hurt and rejected—again—and thinking I was done with reality TV.

That girl in the limo—that was *me*. Raw. Vulnerable. Open. Strong. Independent. Confident that I was meant for something "big," something bold, something better than what I had just experienced.

In that moment of pain, some of the very best parts of me all got pushed to the surface, all at once.

My parents and friends noticed a change in me the moment I got home. The show hadn't aired yet, so no one back home had any idea what had happened. They could assume I didn't get engaged, because Colton never came to our house to meet my family.

But my family picked up on the fact that I was walking in with a confidence that wasn't there when I left; a sort of ownership of who I was, even though I was confused, and disappointed that I'd been rejected by a guy who checked so many boxes on paper, and who I went in believing I could trust. "Wow, you actually stood up for yourself!" they said.

I was broke and tired, but also sort of rejuvenated. All of the journaling I'd done during Colton's season—and that was *a lot*—had me feeling like I was really starting to get to know myself better. And having all of that time to just *think* and really feel out what I wanted . . . well, I wanted to keep going, growing and understanding myself more.

Then the show started airing, and I swear that in front of the camera I looked like a crazy person. And I am a little crazy! I'll admit it. That's what makes me fun! But when I watched the fight between me and Caelynn on TV, it looked way uglier than it actually felt to me when it happened. At one point I growled, like some kind of a lioness or something, and I remember doing that in the context of just joking around about how angry I was. Things I thought were funny because they were a little bit outrageous, things I did just for fun, gave people all kinds ammunition to label me the Crazy Girl on TV.

Social media went nuts over it.

I don't think anyone realized how bad the social-media hatred was gonna get. But it was *bad*. People were taking the time to DM me, calling me the C-word, and telling me I should die. There were four days straight where I just stayed in my pajamas hosting my own pity party. *I'm embarrassed. I can't get on my social media anymore. I'm afraid to go out. I can't do anything.*

That newfound confidence and slowly improving sense of self? Yeah, those took a hit.

But toward the end of the season, I started to grow on people. I became somebody people wanted to root for, and the comments on social media started to change for the better after my final exit. I didn't think I wanted to be the Bachelorette, or that the public would *want* me to be the Bachelorette. But I think the fact that I'd gone through so much, and talked so openly about my feelings—treating my interviews like therapy sessions—made me super relatable to a lot of viewers.

I felt like a lot of young women were in similar places in life.

The more I thought about it, the more I realized how much I'd learned from the experience. It was the first time I was forced in such a huge way to consider the big questions in life: Who am I? What do I want? What is love to me? How have I been hurt? What do I really want and need in a partner, *beyond* what I've put down on paper?

Considering those questions in an extreme situation where I had no phone, no TV, no real friends, no family, not even my own music to listen to—like *Survivor* for love, basically—I had two choices: I could hang out with the other girls and gossip, or I could take some time to look into myself.

I chose to spend a lot of that time looking into myself.

I wrote in my journal a lot that winter, which helped me come to the realization that being the next Bachelorette might actually be what God wanted from me. The more I prayed, the more it seemed clear that it might be a way to get the healing I needed. A way in which showing my imperfections could help others. And *maybe*, hopefully, a way for me to finally find love.

The more I thought about it, the more I wanted it.

I mean, my whole life I'd felt like I was destined to do something big. Maybe this was it, and the Hannah that so many other women saw in the limo was someone I could learn how to be every day. Or maybe this was God's mysterious way of bringing a really good man into my life. My girlfriends in Alabama were all married. Some of 'em already had kids. I was the only one of my close friends who'd somehow managed to make the wrong relationship choices again and again. Maybe I needed something this big, this extreme, to help me get there.

So I went to LA, and I talked with the producers.

I made it to the final round.

This was it. My big interview. My very last chance to make a really good impression.

A part of me still couldn't believe they were even considering me after I came off looking like a psycho on *The Bachelor* (which was still airing when this meeting happened). I wasn't exactly made out to look like a dream girl. But by the time this big meeting came around with the *Bachelor* creator and the head of unscripted TV at ABC, I had fully convinced myself that this was a *good* thing. It was not only my chance to go back on TV and continue to grow, to redeem myself and show the world who I really was, it was also a chance to travel the world and go on dates with a set of hand-picked bachelors from around the country. And probably, hopefully, fall in love with one of them. I mean, how could any girl pass that up?

Which all came to mean that I *wanted* this.

I was pretty positive I wouldn't get it, but I wanted it just the same.

You know how it is when you're going for a big job interview? How you want to be your absolute best? Auditioning for a TV show is kind of like that, only with ten times the pressure to *look* your best. That's just how Hollywood is. There are just so many gorgeous women everywhere. And the producers made it clear that for this final interview, I needed to show up and *be* the Bachelorette. I needed to *"dress* the part, and *look* the part, and *act* the part," they said, and I needed to be open with them "about everything."

So I spent *days* pumping myself up for that interview.

Thankfully it was a good hair day, and my acne was under control. (Finally!) Plus, I found this really cute pink jumpsuit and a nice jacket to wear. I couldn't afford to keep the jacket, so I kept the price tag on it, but it left me feeling pretty confident—until I dropped my lipstick as soon as I got out of the car. As soon as I squatted down to pick it up, I heard *skrrrrrrip!*

Oh no.

I lifted the bottom of my jacket and looked, and sure enough I'd ripped my jumpsuit—right in the center of my butt crack.

Oh, no. No, no, no.

What was I gonna do? I didn't have any other clothes with me.

I went into the building and ran straight to the bathroom. I looked over my shoulder at my reflection in the mirror, and it seemed like the jacket *kinda* covered up some of the hole, but who was I kidding? It was obvious, and there was nothing I could do to fix it. I didn't have time to go back to the hotel to change. There was no way I could tell these executives that I'd be late to my big interview. So I shrugged and walked into the office, feeling about as exposed and ridiculous as a woman could feel.

"Hannah!" they said.

They were all smiles. We shook hands, and they drew attention to my outfit, like, "Wow, that jumpsuit is great!"

I could feel my face turn red with embarrassment.

"Well," I said with an awkward smile, "let me tell you about this jumpsuit. I am coming in here today being *so* open with you guys."

"What do you mean?"

"I have a rip in the seat of my pants right now," I said, laughing out loud.

"What?"

"Yeah, I ripped my jumpsuit in the parking lot," I said as I sat down. It wasn't like a great big *gaping* hole. And I was wearing underwear. So I stood up and said, "Oh, what the heck," and I turned around and lifted my suit jacket to show them, and those men doubled over in laughter.

"See," I said. "*Here I am!* I mean, nobody else is gonna come in here and be as open and vulnerable as I am right now."

By the time we finished, I felt good about the interview, and about being myself, but I left their offices still thinking there was no way those powerful men were gonna pick someone who's this much of a dork.

And so, I tried put it out of my mind.

A month later I was back home in Alabama, sitting on my parents' couch and talking to a camera crew that I thought was there just to scout my hometown in case I was chosen as the Bachelorette. Then my cell phone rang. It was host Chris Harrison, FaceTiming to tell me that if I wanted it, I'd been chosen as the next Bachelorette!

I was floored. I truly thought I'd proven myself way too uncool. I got really emotional about it. With cameras rolling, I was flooded with emotions that I couldn't even understand.

But that night it hit me: Maybe all the emotion I was feeling was because this was about something more than a TV show. Maybe this was about God trying to tell me something He'd been trying to get me to hear for a very long time. Maybe it was about time I stopped worrying about trying to be what I *thought* everybody else wanted. Maybe I should just believe in myself; and maybe I should learn to expect the unexpected and trust that the Lord knows what He's doing. Every time I let go of what I thought people *wanted* from me, and was myself . . . things got better. It was a fact.

I'd resisted that message for a very long time. And unfortunately, I wasn't done resisting it. He'd have to tell me a few more times before I'd fully give in, but that night, after receiving that call and hearing that news, I *heard* Him. I decided to take a leap of faith.

I had no idea just how crazy the next year of my life was about to get.

I had no way of knowing just how far I was gonna stray from my connection to the Lord in the coming year, either.

But that afternoon, I said a little prayer. A prayer I probably should've been praying my whole life, and one I would definitely end up praying again down the road.

"Lord," I said, "I don't understand why you've chosen me for this. I don't understand: Why me? I don't even know if I can handle this ride you're about to put me on. But I trust You. I trust that You know what You're doing. So please, *please*, bless me through this ride."

CHAPTER 16

What Happens in Windmills

I left for LA the same day they told me I'd been chosen.

At the airport, they told me I was going to be on *The Ellen DeGeneres Show*. I'd dreamed about being in the audience of the *Ellen* show some day. I'd watched her and danced in my living room at the top of every show. I had wanted to *be* her for years. I kept thinking, *How is this all happening?*

When we touched down, they put me into three straight days of fittings. I walked into the stylist's home full of racks and racks full of dresses and coats, a kind of luxury I had never even seen before, and I felt completely overwhelmed with fear, doubt, and anxiety as they tried to dress me like a Bachelorette was expected to dress.

Okay, so I'm the Bachelorette, I thought as I looked at myself in the mirror. *But will people like me?*

I broke down crying.

The show had never chosen a Bachelorette who wasn't in the final four of the prior *Bachelor* season. I was coming in as the underdog, and I knew some fans of the show were going to be disappointed about that.

I thought the men might be disappointed, too.

They had all applied and been chosen before knowing I was the girl they'd be pursuing. I knew it was going to be a surprise to them to find out it was me. I struggled with not feeling I was "worthy" to be the Bachelorette. I couldn't even say it. Like, the words wouldn't come out of my mouth: "I'm the Bachelorette."

It felt to me as if they had chosen the wrong Hannah.

A girl named Hannah Godwin was the runner-up for Colton's heart. She is gorgeous. She's another Alabama girl, and is the sort of Insta model every man wants to date.

I'm the other girl. The one who growls and voluntarily eats bugs.

That's what I was feeling when the first limo drove up.

I already told you a little bit about my first two nights on *The Bachelorette*, way back at the very beginning of this book. I mentioned that I was immediately physically attracted to Tyler the moment he stepped out of the limousine. (Whew, that boy was good-looking.) But I was drawn to a few of the other guys on the first night, too. (Spoiler alert: these guys made it to my final four.)

Peter, the dark-haired pilot, had something so nice and charming about him. He showed up in his pilot's uniform, and who doesn't love a man in uniform? I thought it was so sweet when he gave me his wings—the aviator badge that's only issued to pilots. I was intrigued.

I felt a spark with Luke, too, who I had briefly met on "After the Final Rose" at the end of Colton's season. It was refreshing to see a familiar face, especially when we sat down and he told me that he was there to take this seriously and to win my heart. It felt like he was being intentional with me. Like he was 100 percent dialed in. He made it clear in that blue-eyed stare that he was there for *me*. He was a little aggressive about it, wrapping his arm around my back and holding my waist as he spoke to me, but there was something reassuring about how sure he was. (That's why I gave him the first-impression rose—another really big deal, which you know if you're a *Bachelor/Bachelorette* fan.)

And Jed, being a southern boy from Nashville, offered a sense of familiarity as well. Plus, he made a super-fun first impression. I'm a sucker for music, and when he sat down and sang me a song he wrote just for me? *Ahhhh.* Was it cheesy? Yes! But it was fun. I like a guy who can be silly, and the passion of a musician is just hard to pass up.

Honestly, meeting so many men so quickly was overwhelming. The television part was new to me, but really, so was dating. The five men I had kissed in my whole life had all been serious relationships, and the two men I'd slept with were men I loved. I didn't have flings. I didn't have casual sex. I didn't even have casual kisses! I told myself that I was gonna let loose a little bit and have fun on *The Bachelorette*, but I also told myself to stay true to my values.

A big part of that was telling myself that I wouldn't have sex with any of the men on the show. It's basically insinuated that the Bachelors and Bachelorettes are intimate with each other for the first time in the Fantasy Suites, which are special one-on-one overnight dates that happen once the contestants are narrowed down to the final few. But I had never had sex with somebody after only a couple of months of knowing them, and this entire show was shot over eight weeks! There was just no way I would ever feel comfortable enough to do that, I thought. And I really didn't want to have any more sex before marriage, anyway. It had only ended up in heartache for me. At least that's what I told myself. I thought if I fell in love and got engaged to someone at the end of the season, anything that happened after that would be up to the two of us, when there weren't any cameras around. And if we were going to be married? Well, maybe then we could talk about it.

As you know if you've seen the show, my promises to myself basically flew out the window.

I wound up kissing more men in one night than I'd kissed in my whole life. And I was surprised to find that it was *fun*. Over the course of the next few weeks, I kissed guys I might have never dated if I stayed in Alabama. I kissed men who weren't my type, and I liked it! I also kissed men who I thought I didn't want to kiss at all. As the people in charge, including host Chris Harrison, kept reminding me, they were making a TV show, and they needed me to "trust the process."

Going outside my comfort zone was part of the adventure.

But man, it was exhausting.

Television production schedules are demanding. As the lead in the show, I was always on camera, which meant that the show kept me working all the time.

One morning in the first couple of weeks, I actually passed out on the way to get my makeup done. They took me to a hospital just to be safe, and I ended up being treated for exhaustion and dehydration (they showed part of this on Week 3), but as soon as I came out of the hospital, we had to keep filming to stay on schedule. Always the trooper, I got right back to work.

We were always rushing from one place to the next, and in between they were interviewing me on camera to get my impressions of everything that had just happened. I was surrounded by all of this beauty, but I hardly got a chance to enjoy it because we were at work. *The Bachelor* shows took me to eight different countries by the time

I was finished: Singapore, Thailand, Vietnam, the Netherlands, Scotland, Latvia, Greece, and then Mexico—where I made a guest appearance on *Bachelor in Paradise*—and I didn't really get to experience any of them the way I had hoped.

I mean, I went bungee jumping, pretty much naked, with somebody I haven't talked to since. That's weird, right? That's not a normal dating experience. It's not a normal life experience! It was cool, but it's not exactly a comfortable date with somebody who's basically a stranger.

It looks like it's all glamorous on TV. Believe me, I thought that's what it would be. But it was *hard*. The lack of sleep and loss of contact with the outside world made me feel like I was losing my mind at times. There were days when I honestly couldn't see straight, or think straight, but I kept going because I didn't want to let anyone down. Especially myself.

It was week after week of some of the most intense experiences I've ever had—some of them amazing, which many people don't get to experience in a lifetime, let alone a couple of months, and which I'll treasure forever. I met a lot of great people, too. But that time period between March 3, when they first told me I was the new Bachelorette, through May, when we finished filming, and what happened in the weeks after the show started airing, were also some of the biggest emotional roller-coaster rides I've ever been on. I mean, even if you love roller coasters, if you ride them one after the other all day long every day for weeks on end, you might feel a little woozy!

People have asked me what it feels like to be dating so many men at once, and honestly, for the sake of the TV show, I learned to sort of turn off my feelings from one date to the next. If I had a great date with one of the guys, I would just shut those feelings down when it was over and put all of my attention into the next date. I wanted the guys to be comfortable, and the only way I could do that was to give them my full attention, so they would be real with me.

It was good for the show, I think. But it wasn't necessarily good for figuring out what my heart really wanted.

One of the big differences between participating in one of these shows as a contestant and being the lead was that I didn't have time to write in my journal. I no longer had any time to slow down, to really process how I was feeling, and how what I was feeling related to what I actually wanted. Even my interviews were more about narrating and explaining what was happening than they were about processing my feelings. So I didn't get any of that therapy-like feeling I'd had on *The Bachelor*.

I was getting paid for *The Bachelorette*, too, so it really was a "job." The people in charge were my bosses, and we were all responsible for making a season of extremely valuable television. There was a lot of pressure on everybody to get it right, and the spotlight of *all* of that pressure on *me*.

Something about being in that position made me go right back to my default setting of trying to be the "best" in the eyes of other people. (Funny how sometimes trying to be the "best" makes you feel the worst.) I wanted to make a really good TV show, but I also wanted to have a real experience, and to find true love.

That wasn't the best combo for my heart.

Trying to do both of those things at once meant that there were times when I had to go against my intuition, to go against my gut, and to almost force myself to feel true feelings for men whom I didn't have much more than a little crush on.

At the beginning, when I couldn't see my husband in the room, I thought, *Okay, I'm going to have faith.* And, at some point down the line, the more I got to know the guys, the more I convinced myself there was really *was* something there with the men I chose going into the final four.

✳

If you didn't watch my season and you want to know everything that happened on the show, by all means go watch it. (You should probably watch it before you keep reading, 'cause I'm about to give away some massive spoilers!)

I don't want to rehash everything that happened. But I do want to talk about some of the big stuff. Looking back on it, what happened with the final four were matters of the heart. My *real* heart. The one that I would have no choice but to tend to long after this TV show was over.

After weeks of traveling and group dates and one-on-ones, my attraction to Peter Weber had grown like crazy. He was just so sweet, and I was developing some really strong feelings for him. But I was frustrated, because we never seemed to have enough time together to actually *talk*. On some of the other dates on the show, there was downtime when the camera crews and lighting crews were busy getting ready to shoot, when I would get a few minutes to talk to my dates off camera. I enjoyed some of those off-camera talks more than the on-camera ones, since it felt like we were really getting to know each other like we might in everyday life. But for some reason, that almost never happened with Peter.

Which leads me to the whole windmill situation.

By the time we got to Greece, and the show put us up in our Fantasy Suite in the base of a rustic old-stone windmill, we were just hungry for some alone time to get to know each other on a more personal level.

Neither one of us went in there thinking we were going to have sex. It was weird at first. I carried my Sulley pillow with me. It took a while to remember that we could talk openly, and that neither one of us was wearing a microphone. We played cards for a while, and he taught me this magic trick that his grandfather had taught him, which he said he had never taught anybody before. And I don't know if it was a release from all the pressure I'd been under, or a result of all the intensity of dating and kissing so many men at the same time all those weeks, or if it was just our natural chemistry together, but once we got really comfortable and connected with each other, we got into that little double bed between the stone walls, and one thing led to another.

It was intimate, and fun. And we promised not to tell anyone about it, because we wanted to keep it real. This wasn't something we did for the cameras, or the show, or the fans. We both said we wanted to keep it between us.

I had never slept with anybody so quickly in a relationship, ever, and the morning after my Fantasy Suite night with Peter I definitely felt some good-girl guilt about it. I was conflicted, because I really *did* have feelings for Peter. I was definitely falling in love with him. I just hadn't had enough time to know for sure if what I felt for him was real, and I was worried I didn't have much time left to decide whether I wanted to have a life with this man. With *any* of the men, really.

Three nights later, in another Fantasy Suite, I had sex with Jed, too. He was the one who felt safe to me. He was the first one I told I was falling in love with him.

I went into the room with Jed with pretty much the exact same expectations I'd had with Peter: I was just looking forward to alone time away from the cameras. But it was maybe more complicated with Jed, because we had this deep emotional connection. I loved that he had grown up in the South, and had a bit of that southern charm, but in a modern way, with a more modern perspective on things. Like me!

He'd made a point of admitting to me earlier on that his primary reason for coming on *The Bachelorette* was not to find love but to promote his career as a musician. He wanted to do anything he could to reach a bigger audience, he said. At first I was a little shocked to hear that he hadn't come on the show for *me*, like so many of the other guys had, but then he told me that I had taken him by surprise—and he had fallen for me. Big time. I just thought that was so honest of him. The fact that he had been surprised by his own feelings and was willing to tell me the truth about what he was feeling made me trust him more than ever. And that trust went a long way with me.

We also had some good chemistry going on, and once we started making out, there was no turning back. I'll be honest here: the sex wasn't as good as it was with Peter. But my emotional need for connection was more fulfilled. Our night together felt more like what a date night would feel like back home. We had music, and space to dance, and we prayed, and we talked about our relationship with God. Jed and I had spent more time together off camera already, and I already felt more natural and comfortable around him. But in this one night I got to experience what it might feel like to be together in the real world, not just in a tiny bed between stone walls.

That was it for me. I made up my mind right there.

The emotional connection, the familiarity, that sense that we had similar backgrounds, that we could *build* something together—after being with Jed, I knew that I wasn't going to sleep with the other two men. I felt pretty confident I knew who I wanted to wind up with. I wanted the guy who would be my best friend, who would make me laugh all the time. Who was *safe*.

A couple of nights later, I went on my overnight date with Luke, and it quickly turned into a nightmare. I had already seen some red flags. His jealousy, the stories of the fights he was getting into with the other guys in the house, the way he seemed to want to control what I was doing even when he wasn't around me—none of it felt right. But when it came to values, I thought he and I were the most aligned. He was a Christian, and a "born-again virgin" who talked openly about his faith. That was still up at the top of my list of qualities that I wanted in a future husband, just as it had been when I dated Colton on *The Bachelor*. And I truly believed what he said: he was there to meet me, and wanted to be with me. That felt right. That felt safe to me.

But that night, after weeks of telling me that he loved me, Luke *insisted* on knowing if I had slept with any of the other guys. He *insisted* that I had to tell him, even though I clearly didn't want to talk about it. (It was written all over my face.) And when I asked him why he was so adamant, he said that if I *had* slept with any of the other guys on the show, even one of them, then he wanted "to go home"— which is *Bachelor*-speak for "I want to break up with you."

I got angry.

I understood that somebody who was in love with me might be uncomfortable or upset if I had been intimate with somebody else. Of *course* that wouldn't be the easiest thing to hear. It's not fun to have to worry about that when you care for somebody, and if he had addressed it in that way, it might have resulted in more compassion and connection between us. But the way he worded it, it seemed more like he was concerned about how me being intimate with any of the other guys meant I wasn't "on the same page" as him in terms of being a Christian. Like he wanted to shame me for "slipping up." And that was not okay with me.

We weren't in an exclusive relationship. By definition, because I was dating multiple men at the same time on this show, we weren't all the way there in terms of commitment to each other. Trying to control me and/or my relationships with other men at that stage was over the line.

Plus, we had already been on a lousy date that day in Santorini. He kept making comments that hurt my feelings. (Like complaining about my breath after we'd both just eaten gyros. Trust me, his breath was bad, too!) I felt like he'd ruined my chance to enjoy that beautiful island, which was a place that was on my bucket list. And I had given him so many second chances already, while trying to figure out why he was the way he was. He was so full of pride, and competitiveness, and so full of aggression toward the other guys, and I had been *so* patient and understanding with him.

But I swear, when he said those things, it was like I was staring Brady in the face all over again. The person that I had foolishly loved with everything in my heart since I was in high school had told me that he couldn't see me as his wife anymore because I'd had sex with somebody else. And now Luke was sitting in front of me, essentially saying the same narrow-minded, misogynistic, one-sided BS. And the overwhelming thought that came bubbling up like hot lava was, *How* dare *you?*

So I let him have it. "You're not my husband," I said.

"Can I cut you off for a second?" he asked.

"No," I said flatly. "You're questioning me and you're judging me when I don't feel like you have a right to at this point."

"Guess what?" I said to him. "Sex might be a sin out of marriage. Pride is a sin, too. And I feel like this is a pride thing for you."

He went on trying to explain himself, admitting that he did not have a right to ask me that and trying to speak over me, and I said, "I'm a grown woman and can make my own decisions, and I'm *not* strapped to a man right now!"

I would've expected someone who wanted to be my husband to be less judgmental. But Luke just kept trying to mansplain to me what it means to be "on the same page" about our faith, before he even knew for sure if I had slept with anyone else. It was so controlling, and so wrong of him to devalue everything about me because of that one thing.

So much of my time on the show was spent trying to understand Luke, the connection we had, and why it was just so dang hard. And in that moment, I saw for sure that the two of us didn't have a future.

So I told him: "I feel like I have finally gotten clarity on you, and I do not want you to be my husband."

Still, he would not give up. He wouldn't get into the car to go home. So I finally just came out and told him. "I *have* had sex," I said. "And Jesus still loves me."

Even *then* he refused to get into the car, so I got even more explicit: I used the F-word to describe what Peter and I had done in the windmill, and I told Luke that after everything he'd said, "probably, you want to leave."

I had no intention of breaking my promise to Peter. I wanted to keep what we'd done a secret—but my emotions and temper got the best of me. And it was all captured on camera.

In what felt like a final moment of personal judgment, Luke then asked, "Can I pray over you?"

"No," I said.

And that was it. He got into the car with his head down, and I tried to move on with my life. As you know if you watched the show, he wouldn't let it go. He came back and tried to convince me to give him yet another shot. At that point, his behavior reminded me of Tucker's. And I was over it.

That was a big moment for me. He was acting just like these other people who had hurt me in my past, but instead of putting up with it, I ended it.

Standing up for myself with Luke felt like I had finally conquered something I couldn't always do in my past relationships. I wouldn't let him shame me. I wouldn't let him turn it back on me. I wouldn't let his "I love yous" and "I'm sorrys" pull me back in. I just wouldn't.

It didn't matter that we had similarities. It didn't matter that I felt a little spark for him right from the start. Luke wasn't right for me, and this time I put me first.

My final Fantasy Suite date before moving into the show's finale was with Tyler—the man I expected to send home next.

Now, when it comes to physical attraction, if there was anybody on that show who grabbed my attention, it was *him*. He had the sort of bad-boy good looks that scared me and intrigued me at the same time. It wasn't love at first sight, it was more like lust at first sight. And because I'd been down that road before (with Tucker, and with Brady), I knew he had the power to hurt me.

That made me nervous.

I knew from the beginning that I needed to be careful. I mean, we had *chemistry*. I loved making out with him. He made me blush. I didn't understand why he liked me, and I feared I could really like him. But while he could charm, I kept wondering, What was his angle? I let him get close, but not too close. It seemed too risky. What if I fell for him and he was just in it for fame? Would he reject me?

I had started to soften slowly over the course of our time on the show, but things really had started to change for me when I met his family the week before this. I remember feeling like they were my people. We just clicked. And then my family met him and loved him, too. And that made me wonder if maybe I had been falling in love with him all along.

What I needed from the Fantasy Suite date was to get to know him—to see if it was safe for me to fall for him. And that is exactly what we did. We connected that night like two people might at the beginning of a long romance. We bonded like close friends do, just talking and talking for hours. We talked about family, and about all sorts of things that were so personal that we didn't want to share them with each other on camera.

After that night together, when we were completely open with each other and we made out like crazy—and nothing more—I woke up thinking, *I cannot lose him.*

It was all so confusing. I needed more time with him.

According to the rules of the show, I had to send someone home. I had already brought four people to the Fantasy Suite dates, when past Bachelorettes had only brought three. I had to make up my mind.

How could I send Peter home? We'd had sex! We had such a wonderful night together. Sending him home would shock him, and maybe break his heart. That was confusing to me, too.

Of these three men who I had just started to develop genuine feelings for, Jed was the only one who didn't feel so confusing to me. Our relationship had at least progressed on somewhat of a natural timeline. And at that point, just that little bit of extra familiarity felt safer than anything else.

CHAPTER 17

Losing Trust

I've spent a lot of time looking back on this crazy-fast period of my life, and trying to make sense of the decisions I made—including the bad ones. And I think it all comes down to this: because I had no internal peace, I was looking for external signs to help me make my decisions. At that point, I had zero internal confidence in my ability to decide what was right or wrong, and after the Fantasy Suite date nights, I had only five days to decide which guy I wanted to potentially marry. I had already disregarded so many of my gut feelings just to get through the making of the show that I was physically, mentally, and spiritually exhausted.

So I looked outside myself for signs from God, from the universe, from other people's opinions, from anything I could get. And whenever I was with Jed, I saw signs.

For example, every time I was on a date with Jed, I saw dream catchers. Even in the Netherlands, which to me seemed like the last place a person might see a dream catcher on some random wall. Dream catchers always made me feel safe, and for a girl who was looking for markers from God, that seemed like a pretty clear sign. It seemed like maybe my aunt and cousins were trying to let me know that *they* knew the person I was supposed to be with.

So even though things were complicated, the signs I saw made me feel like my heart was being led to Jed. And I ignored the mixed emotions in my gut saying maybe, just maybe, I didn't have enough information to make the decision.

I had to send someone home the morning after I woke up with Tyler, and I decided it had to be Peter. It felt brutal sending him home. Like we'd just started really falling for each other, and then *bam*, it was over. He had no idea it was coming. None! I felt terrible. I'm not someone who spends a night with a guy, gets so intimate with him, and then tosses him to the curb a few days later. That wasn't *me*. Or at least that's not who I wanted to be. I had just changed my mind about it a few hours before I let him go, so I wasn't even sure about it myself. He was upset. I was upset.

The pressure was like nothing I'd ever felt before, and I didn't feel like I knew any of these guys well enough to fully make up my mind.

You know what it felt like? It felt like MASH, the fortune-telling game that my friends and I used to play in the after-school pickup line. You can look up a detailed description of this game on YouTube, but MASH stands for Mansion, Apartment, Shack, House, and you write down options and then randomly connect all these things in your imaginary future life, like the city you're going to live in, the boys you have crushes on, the number of kids you're going to have. And then, depending on the list and the way the game plays out, the result predicts your life: "You're gonna live in a shack with your second crush, Bobby, and have five kids, and you're going to drive a minivan!"

In this case, the theoretical game eliminated the choices until I got down to, "Well, I guess it's Jed!"

I took ownership over my decision. It wasn't decided by chance or by anyone else. But my mom later said I was making decisions like a little kid might: "Oh, I'll take that one because his sister Lily has the same birthday as Patrick! And he wrote me four songs, and he broke a string on his guitar and made me a cute bracelet out of it!" All of those things are true, by the way, but these aren't reasons to get engaged to somebody. They all seem kind of silly, looking back on it now.

But then? All I saw were the signs I needed.

I sent Tyler home about forty minutes before Jed was scheduled to arrive.

I hated it. We had all this potential that hadn't been fully explored yet, but there just wasn't time.

According to the signs and the experiences I'd had over those crazy eight weeks, Jed was the guy who I thought could give me a life I wanted.

So as I stood on a beautiful hillside in Greece, waiting for Jed to arrive, the air felt charged, in an exciting way.

Everyone around me already knew that I was about to hand him the final rose; and if/when he got down on one knee to propose to me, they were pretty sure I was going to say yes.

It was beautiful. The sun was starting to get lower in the sky. There was a herd of goats on the hillside. (Of course, having goats around meant there was goat poop everywhere. The bottoms of my shoes were covered in it by the end of the night! But I digress . . .)

Jed walked up, carrying his guitar, and I was all nervous and giddy. It was all so beautiful, and I had such deep feelings for Jed at this point. My smile was real when I gave him the final rose. He deserved it. We were *good* together. We could build a life together in Tennessee. I could see that future, at his home, with his dog, listening to him sing and write songs—even though it all felt a bit premature.

I was caught up in the magic and the fantasy of it all when all of a sudden he got down on one knee and pulled out a ring, and I thought . . . *No. I can't. This isn't what it is supposed to be like.*

I said yes anyway.

It's hard to explain how conflicted I felt. Jed hadn't done anything wrong. I cared about him. And the engagement itself was dreamy— but it wasn't necessarily *my* dream. This wasn't what I thought it would feel like when I said "Yes" to a man with the intention of spending the rest of my life with him.

Still, that's exactly what I did. I didn't listen to my intuition. I set my gut feeling aside, and I said "Yes."

My smile was not a lie. I wanted to be with Jed. I was excited to have more alone time with him. I thought I loved him. I *did*. But even as we hugged and kissed each other, as the goats ran out on that beautiful hillside in that gorgeous setting and everything looked so perfect, I kept thinking, *This doesn't feel the way I know love feels.*

Well, I thought, *maybe it'll just take time.*

There never seemed to be enough time.

So I focused on that: we'd have time now to fall into the love that we'd started on *The Bachelorette.*

✳

I didn't realize until afterward what the date of our engagement was. I didn't realize until after that Neil Lane diamond was on my finger that the day we got engaged was the very same day as the anniversary of my aunt's and cousins' murder.

It didn't occur to me until a few weeks later that maybe all those dream catchers I saw weren't signs that Jed was *the one*. Maybe those dream catchers were a warning. Maybe they were signs that Jed wasn't the man for me at all.

✳

The show rented a nice house for us to share after our engagement—our first Happy Couple Retreat—but it was a long trip from the resort where I had already been staying, and I was tired. "Let's just stay here tonight," I said, and Jed was fine with that. We went to my room, which was beautiful, and we spent the night together, and it was great. We were so happy to be alone with each other again.

Our blissful time off camera wouldn't last long, though. First thing in the morning I had to get up and go back on camera for ITMs—In the Moment shots, as they're known in the industry—where I would be asked how much I missed Tyler, and how hard it was to say goodbye, while Jed got to go off and play some golf. It was only a day later. I wasn't really "missing" Tyler yet. But I wanted to know if he was okay, and when they told me that he was upset, it upset me. I still cared about him. And if he still cared about me, did that mean I'd made a wrong decision? Peter was apparently really upset, too, and I couldn't let go of the question of what might have happened if I'd had more time to get to know *both* of them.

That night Jed and I moved to the big rental house, where we had the privacy of a whole second-floor suite to ourselves. The very next day, the show would start airing in the United States. I would fly to New York to do press the morning after that, while Jed would get to fly home.

So much for "time."

All Jed and I would be allowed to spend together before we had to say goodbye were those three nights. After that, we would be forced to stay apart for the next three months so we wouldn't spoil the TV show. I couldn't even put his name in my phone, for fear somebody might see it when he called me and then leak it to the press. (I gave him the name "Ricky Bobby" in my contacts. Yes, that's Will Farrell's character from *Talladega Nights*.) I would only get a chance to see him in secret a handful of times while the show aired, and it would take a whole clandestine operation to pull that off.

Those two nights in the rental house felt really important to me, so we could get our engagement started right—and they didn't start well at all. On the first night after our engagement, Jed made a comment that caught me off guard.

"I just think it's really cool that I'm engaged to you," he said, "and you knew that was gonna happen, and you weren't intimate with anybody else. I'm glad I don't have to worry about that."

"Wait," I said. "What do you mean?"

"You said you weren't intimate with anybody except me," he repeated.

I remembered telling him at some point after our overnight date that he was the one; I wasn't going to be with anybody else. But in the blur of everything, I couldn't even remember when I said it.

"No, Jed," I said. "I told you after our night, I knew it was you and I wasn't intimate with anyone *after* you."

That caught *him* off guard.

196

"Was I not the first person?" he asked.

"No. I had my date with Peter first."

"And you two were . . ."

I nodded, and he got up and started pacing the room, asking all sorts of questions.

I explained again what had happened, and he wanted details. He wanted to know if he was better in bed than Peter, and I lied and said "Yes." I didn't want to bruise his ego any more than it was already bruised.

He also asked me if his *thing* was bigger than Peter's. Why do guys always ask that? "I don't even remember," I told him. I just didn't see how answering that question would be good for anybody.

Here's the thing: to me, when you're in love, when you're connected emotionally, none of that stuff matters. Sex is a whole different thing when you're connected by the heart. It truly is. I hated that this was happening. I hated that he was feeling jealous about it all. I was battling all sorts of internal guilt and shame over everything that had happened myself. I let these fleeting feelings lead to making choices that affected a lot of people. I didn't take the time, and there wasn't enough time, for me to think through all of the consequences. There was a lot of hurt going around because of the choices I'd made, and I was worried Jed was going to say the horrible words I'd already heard from two other men in my life: that because of this, he would think I was unworthy of his love.

But he didn't say it.

"I chose you," I reminded him. "I *choose* you."

After fifteen minutes of pacing, Jed calmed down.

We spent the night together, and things seemed to go back to normal, even though we didn't know what "normal" really meant for us at that point.

The next day, we hung out by the pool and drank and had fun all day.

After dinner I went to take a shower, and as I was getting out, Jed came in, looking visibly upset about something. I asked him what was wrong. We sat on the bed together. He said he had just talked to one of the producers and learned that there was a girl spreading a story online, about the two of them hanging out together just before he came on the show.

I didn't get upset at first. There were always rumors on social media from past girlfriends or boyfriends or other people trying to get attention for themselves once somebody made it to the final four on one of these shows. So I didn't think it was that much of a big deal.

"What do you mean, hanging out? Like, what does that mean? Was she your girlfriend?"

"No, no, no. She wasn't my girlfriend. We just hung out."

"I don't even understand, then. Why didn't you tell me?"

"It was nothing worth telling you."

But he still looked upset about it.

"I have to go do press tomorrow," I said, "and if they're gonna ask me about this, I need to know if there's something to talk about. Like, what is it? When's the last time you talked to her? Was it a month? Was it a week? When was it?"

At first he said a month. Then he said maybe it was more like a week.

"Oh, my gosh, Jed. Okay. But you weren't *anything* with her?"

"No. We just hung out. That's it."

He stuck to his story, and I took him at his word.

Before we headed to the airport for our flights back to the US, one of our handlers was going over Jed's ticket information and she read his name out loud: "Jared Thomas Wyatt."

"Jared?" I said. "Who's *Jared*?"

It freaked me out. How could I not know my fiancé's full name? Who *was* this person?

I asked Jed, "Why didn't I know your name?"

"I never went by that," he said. He didn't think it was a big deal. But alongside everything else, it just made me question whether *any* of this was real.

How could I be engaged to a man when I didn't even know his name?

And his name was . . . *Jared*?

✳

I went back to the States to face a whirlwind of press. The pressure never let up. The only real sleep I got was on the plane. And then I was hidden away, so I wouldn't get ambushed by the paparazzi and there wasn't a chance that I'd slip up and give away any spoilers.

Away from the cameras, the pressure and the worry of it all was too much for me. I started drinking more than I ever had in my whole life. I didn't want to drink more, but I felt like I needed something. I was self-medicating. And I knew that wasn't good for me.

In one of our very few chances to see each other in person a few weeks later, the show secretly took Jed and me to a California hideaway for a Happy Couple Retreat. It was so good to see each other, and hold each other, and reconnect for three days straight. I remembered why I'd chosen him, and why I said yes.

I said yes because we had fun together. We got silly and built a fort in the living room, like a couple of kids. We tied sheets to chairs and tables, and crawled under it, and made a video on my phone, looking so blissfully happy.

I said yes because Jed seemed like the safest choice.

I even wrote it in my journal:

He comes from a southern background. He is safe.

He is Christian. He is safe.

We know a lot about each other. He's safe . . .

After the whirlwind of two TV shows back-to-back; after the whirlwind of dating more guys in two months than a lot of women date in a lifetime; after kissing more men in one night than I'd kissed in my life and sleeping with two men in one week; after dealing with the pressure and hatred and adoration on social media; after answering ten billion questions from the press, all wanting to know answers to things I couldn't tell them without giving anything away—at that point, I *needed* safe. I wanted comfortable. I wanted familiarity.

I'm not gonna lie, I still had feelings for Tyler and Peter. I felt like I had just started to get to know them. And I liked both of them. But neither of them represented what I knew, and that scared me. A pilot who lives in California? I knew nothing about that life. Tyler's home in Florida seemed closer and more familiar, but then he worked in New York City, in construction and modeling. I couldn't picture what life with either one of them might look like.

I could still picture a life with Jed, but it was complicated. I was so anxious a lot of the time. The show was airing. He kept asking about my feelings for Peter and Tyler, and I was honest with him. I did still have feelings for them. He didn't like that. It caused all kinds of arguments between us. I kept second-guessing my decisions, and tried reminding myself that there were *signs*. Good signs. But the worry and the panic was starting to eat me alive.

Well, guess what? All of my worry was warranted.

The night before we left our retreat, the show got a phone call alerting them that *People* magazine was set to run a story the next day—about Jed's "girlfriend."

And on the way back to LA, while I was riding in the back of a car, a friend of mine texted me the hard truth: the *People* story didn't just claim that Jed had a girlfriend. They *interviewed* her. She spoke on the record. She gave them her name. This wasn't some anonymous source on social media.

I was so embarrassed. How could I be finding out about all of this at the same time as the rest of the world?

According to what the girl told *People*, she and Jed had last seen each other the night before he left to be on the show. She claimed that Jed had spoken with her mother. (Which only proved how serious the relationship was. You don't speak to the mother of someone you've only "hung out" with.) And the last thing Jed said to her before the producers took his phone away was "I love you."

Lesson: just because you can picture a life with someone doesn't mean that it's right.

I sat in silence the whole two-hour drive. I didn't cry. I think I was in shock.

Jed and I had talked about this girl a few times in between, and every time, his story changed a little bit. He knew this girl. They were friends. They had been to the Bahamas together, but just as friends. He had told her he loved her, but he was drunk at the time.

Guess what? That's gaslighting. That constantly changing story, making me doubt what I was hearing and thinking, telling half-truths and untruths while making me feel bad for questioning anything— that is the opposite of being sincere, honest, and trustworthy. Why was I allowing guys to do this to me? I mean, if you've read this far, you can't help but see that this wasn't the first time a guy had been less than honest with me. But I was just starting to see that pattern myself.

He said he loved me, and only me, and I kept giving him the benefit of the doubt.

I was so honest with him about how I was feeling, always trusting that he was doing the same, that I made myself vulnerable in what turned out to be an unsafe way. And now?

Once the *People* article came out, *everything* came out. This girl posted actual text messages from Jed, showing for sure that they had been together the night before he came on the show. He had not only said, "I love you," but he had told her that he would call her as soon as he got back from the show.

I wanted to disappear. I couldn't, but I wanted to. I had tried so hard in this experience to put myself out there, and to find out all of this just broke me. This guy I thought I knew had betrayed my trust, and the whole world knew it.

It turns out he had straight up lied to me, and I could not be with a liar.

"I didn't lie to you, Hannah," he begged me. "I just didn't tell you all the details. I didn't want to hurt you."

"Well, by not telling me, you hurt me worse," I said.

Hiding something in order to "not hurt my feelings" is still un-truthful. It's trying to have your cake and eat it too, and while it might benefit *you* in the short term, this is exactly the kind of behavior that ruins relationships. Forever.

✳

When I broke up with Jed, the cameras captured it all. But he seemed to walk away from that conversation with the hope that we might still get back together.

I called him later to make it clear: that wasn't going to happen. He got mad at me for breaking up with him once and for all over the phone, but I just could not bear to see him. I felt so ashamed and just plain stupid for falling for the same old thing from another guy. By misrepresenting his intentions, he'd stolen the chance I had to find love with Tyler, or maybe with Peter. It was unfair to them. It was unfair to every single guy who came on that show with true intentions.

I also felt like I was letting everyone down. All the viewers who had watched this show and invested so much time watching this love story develop were going to be disappointed now. I hated that. But I couldn't say anything about it.

Once again, my heart was broken. But I couldn't say it out loud.

We stopped doing press, which meant that no one in the public got to hear my side of the story as it was happening.

CHAPTER 18
LOSING FAITH

Back in LA, I started to question why I'd gotten engaged at all. Why had I put myself in a position of so much scrutiny? Why had I allowed myself to become the Bachelorette in the first place? And why had everything gotten so messed up?

I blamed myself for caring more about other people's expectations than my own feelings. My own wants.

It was the same thing I had done in the pageant world—the very same thing that led to me *losing*.

In relationships, I did the same thing. I went along with things, or let things go too far, because I wanted a boy to love me. I wanted to be accepted. I wanted to prove I was good. I wanted to be admired.

I treated TV the same way. I wanted to be the good Bachelorette. I wanted to be loved not just by the men but by America. So I followed advice and ignored my gut instincts.

I didn't guard my heart.

I knew I needed help, but I didn't know how to ask.

Thankfully, sometimes in life you don't have to. Help finds *you*.

Right after I found out—along with everybody else—about Jed's girl-friend, which was a few weeks before our engagement aired on TV, I was invited to a women's conference at Oasis Church in LA. Their lead pastor had spoken at my church in Alabama one time, and I remembered her sermon well, so I decided to go.

Some of the women at church recognized me from the show, and they said things like, "I *love* your season!"

"Oh, just wait," I told them. "It's about to get . . . *interesting*."

They decided they wanted to pray for me, and all of a sudden some of my favorite speakers and authors and all of these amazing women were *praying* over me!

It was exactly what I needed.

I needed reassurance that God still had my back, and I got plenty of it that weekend.

This was right before the overnight dates started airing on the show. So nobody in the public or at church knew about any of that yet.

It was hard watching the show and not being able to tell anyone else. I felt so isolated and alone, watching myself on dates with Peter and Tyler, and seeing how sweet and caring they were, and not being able to tell anybody how that felt now that I was so full of regret.

And on top of it all, I was worried. I had no idea how the show was going to present my blowup with Luke without letting the whole world know who I'd had sex with. But either way, showing a fight about faith and sex on TV was going to get a lot of people talking, I thought. And I wasn't sure what people's reaction was going to be.

The studio allowed me to watch the episodes two days before they aired. The idea was to give me time to prepare for my press interviews, so I'd be able to answer questions with authority, while still making sure not to give away any spoilers for the following weeks. What they showed me was always a final cut of the show, with no opportunity to edit it. That meant I had two days' notice on *exactly* what was going to be broadcast to the world.

I was still in LA, sitting alone in a borrowed apartment in West Hollywood, when I watched the episode and realized that the show revealed *everything*.

I sat there, watching me on a TV screen admitting to Luke that I'd had sex in a windmill, and winkingly telling a camera during ITMs that Peter and I had done it twice, and telling Luke that Jesus still loved me—they showed *all of it*.

I couldn't believe it. I knew I had signed up for a reality television show. I knew I was putting myself out there. But talking about sex before marriage in the abstract was one thing. Talking specifically about who I'd had sex with, revealing that to the world, and showing the profanity I used in anger toward the end of a long, extended, frustrating fight with Luke, was something different.

As soon as I saw it, I texted the only person I knew who could possibly do something about it: "Just watched the episode. Kinda hard to watch. My problem is with the F in the windmill part. I don't know if that's necessary with the ongoing sex-shaming from my fellow Christians." I'd already been shamed on social media for naked bungee jumping and kissing so many men.

"I'm freaking out," I continued.

After a long back-and-forth, and a reminder that they couldn't change the show now even if they wanted to, I was told: "Own it Hannah. You speak for millions of women. Speak."

I wound up in a fetal position on the floor, bawling my eyes out and shaking. How could this be happening? How can I fix this?

The fact that I might be speaking for other women was great. But what was this going to do to *me*? I knew that this was going to add fuel to a fire that was already out of my control.

My *parents* were going to see this. My friends back home. My old boyfriends were watching! My old teachers. Half my town. Half my state was watching. People all over the *world* were going to see this intensely personal—and private!—moment play out. I was *panicked*.

People familiar with the show tried to reassure me: "It's going to be good." "You come across as the voice of women grappling with their sexuality and beliefs." They told me I was continuing to be the feminist, the powerful, decisive woman that people reacted to so strongly at the end of my *Bachelor* run. "Believe in yourself." "Trust us!" "It's going to be great!"

Great? Sure, I'd had sex, but it wasn't a casual thing. It wasn't something I had peace about—especially right at that moment! I wasn't nearly as confident about it as the show was making it look, and I knew it was going to make a lot of people really upset. I was glad it might be freeing for a lot of women to see me handle things this way on TV, but privately, I wrestled with it.

I knew that Jesus really *did* still love me. He forgives us our sins. That doesn't mean we should feel free to go out and "sin" all the time. But it also isn't for anyone else to publicly judge me or tell me what's a "sin" or not. It's between me and God.

The way I see it, the Lord is not telling me in a big angry voice, "Don't have sex before marriage because I want it to be that way!" It's more like a caution, because He doesn't want me to ever hurt. And the more I open myself up to another person in an emotional, physical way before we've committed to each other, the more I'm potentially allowing hurt to come into my life through somebody who's not ready to really love me.

In my own attempt to make sense of it all, to feel *okay* about it, I turned to my old, tattered Bible, and I looked at the story of a woman who committed adultery. She was about to be stoned by the people of her town when Jesus showed up and said, "Let he who is without sin cast the first stone."

Of course, everybody looked around, and there wasn't a one of them who was without sin. So they set their rocks down.

I believe what that passage is trying to tell us is it's not our place to judge others—and that includes the judging of ourselves. Jesus was there for her, and He told her He did not condemn her. "Go now and leave your life of sin," He said. He gave her another chance, to do better; and for those who were about to condemn her to do better, too.

Here's the thing: I want to be a sex-positive person. I believe that sex is something that is good, natural, and healthy. But I struggle with intimacy, for all kinds of reasons. And for me, choosing to have sex with people without love and commitment can hurt. I was realizing the hurt of it, and the repercussions of it, all over again. And the shame that was being laid upon me made it even worse.

If people could have seen my heart before that episode of television ever aired, they would have seen that it was already damaged. There was a bruise here, and a gash here, and a stitch over there. And I had only slept with four people in my whole life. I just knew that my heart had been hurt by relationships and men so much, in so many different ways. And the hurt didn't seem to go away.

I was on the journey of making sense of all of that when the Luke episode aired on TV—and it seemed like the whole Christian community turned against me.

I had thirteen thousand comments on my Instagram that night, and almost all of them were slut-shaming me.

By the next day, I had people all over the media shaming me, too. There were some who came out strong on the other side, saying I was a strong, sex-positive woman, just as some people had predicted would happen. But I wasn't either of those things! I was just me! Standing up for myself was good. But I wasn't shouting, "Yeah! I had sex. This is how I live my life!" either.

Still, people in the church shamed me, comment after comment, blog after blog: "Hannah, you've let us all down," "You've been corrupted," "You don't know what your relationship is with the Lord and how important your body is."

Yes, I *did*.

The show aired clips of me being silly before the overnight dates, joking around in front of the camera, saying, "We're gonna get *down!*" I was dancing and goofing, and making sexual innuendos. It was meant to be funny coming out of my mouth. Maybe it would have been funny if the reality of everything that happened hadn't been thrust in front of the audience. Now? It just made me look like somebody I'm not.

And then one of my favorite Christian podcasts, a podcast I'd listened to growing up, talked about me and invited me to come to their church—not because they saw me as a positive public role model but because they questioned my faith.

"Does she really love Jesus with her whole heart?" they asked.

It was so upsetting to me. How in the world could people be saying I was a poor example of Christianity, that I should be ashamed of myself, after witnessing a few minutes of reality TV? I was fighting for my rights and my place as a woman in those moments, and fighting to uphold the strength of my personal relationship with Jesus! Where was the forgiveness? The acceptance?

Because of the whole Jed-breakup situation, I had stopped doing midseason press. So while other people were out there talking about the most personal details of my life, I couldn't comment.

My anxiety was through the roof. I wasn't sleeping. I couldn't go outside and take a walk in a public place for fear that somebody might stop me and talk to me about everything, or scorn me for what I'd done.

I felt like I was in a cage.

*

I flew home to Alabama to try to escape it all and clear my head.

I slept in every day. I cried a whole lot. My mom tried to comfort me, but I didn't want to hear it.

I couldn't understand why God had let me go on these shows and get my heart broken in front of the whole world. What was the purpose of that? And why would He let me be scorned by thousands upon thousands of other believers of my own faith?

I wondered if maybe I had let Him down.

It's almost like I was afraid to talk to God for fear of what He might tell me, so I stopped praying. The shame and hurt took center stage.

I didn't turn my back on God completely. But I definitely pulled away from my connection to faith—just when I needed it the most.

*

The crew, the producers, the executives at ABC—everybody knew what kind of a state I was in. Even some of the most powerful people at the top of the studio reached out to me to see what they could do to help. They expressed that they were sorry that I was having such a rough go of it, and they wanted to make it better.

As all of this was going on, I got a call inviting me to go on *Dancing with the Stars*.

To me, *DWTS* (as it's known in shorthand) sounded like exactly the sort of all-consuming distraction I needed. It sounded like something I could throw myself into, and hopefully, along the way, distract myself from the emotional and spiritual pain I was in.

So I said yes.

This was in July. Rehearsals would be starting in August. Once again, I had no idea what I was getting myself into.

All I knew is I felt like crap. The world kept beating me down, and all I kept thinking about when I looked ahead to that competition show was how much I wanted to win it. I went back and watched clips from prior seasons, and I saw the Mirrorball trophy—like a Super Bowl trophy for ballroom dancing, with a disco ball on top instead of a football—and I *wanted* it. I wanted it *bad*.

I needed a win in my life.

After a year full of humiliating public heartbreak and loss, I wanted to prove to the world—and to myself—that Hannah Brown could still come out on top.

CHAPTER 19

Dancing with the Scars

atching the last two episodes of *The Bachelorette* just before they aired was *brutal*. Me breaking up with Peter, and breaking up with Tyler, and getting engaged to Jed—all of this feeling and heartbreak and doubt and regret that I'd been holding on to the whole summer was about to come out and finally be revealed to the whole world. I was ready for that. But it was just so hard to relive all the pain that I'd been sitting in for all that time, and I didn't feel ready at all to see Jed, Tyler, and Peter again in person.

I didn't talk to Jed again until we saw each other at the "After the Final Rose" special, the live two-night show that aired right after the finale episodes at the very end of July 2019.

The breakup they had filmed aired during that special. It was the first time I had seen it, and our live, in-person reunion that night was just as awkward as it looked. In some ways it felt so good to finally tell the audience, officially, that Jed and I were no longer together. But it was still heartbreaking to come to terms with how it had all ended. It was sad.

Seeing Jed in person, I realized that there were no lingering feelings there at all. I was done with him. I did not miss him. I did not want to be with him. Honestly, it felt like putting it all behind us was already long overdue.

That wasn't the case with Peter and Tyler, though. The best part of the "After the Final Rose" special for me was getting to see them both in person again. I'd been thinking about both of them since the show started airing, and seeing them in person, each on a separate night, definitely let me know that my lingering feelings for them were real.

There was this little twinge of regret at seeing Peter again, wondering what could have happened if we'd had more time. The thing about Peter is that it seemed like he had very real feelings for me. I hadn't doubted that, but I wished we could have had another shot to get to know each other. Still, it seemed pretty definite that he'd be the next Bachelor. There was already a lot of buzz about it, so I didn't really see any future with him as still being on the table. It felt like the best thing to do was to talk him up, and, well, since I had already admitted that we'd had sex twice, I decided to admit to having sex *four times* in the windmill.

I just figured it was over. He was ready to find someone else to be his wife now. And by this time, I had nothing to hide. So I spoke my truth, straight from the heart.

I was still interested in finding a husband, too. I told the live audience I didn't *need* to find a husband. There's a big difference between needing something and wanting it. Wanting it, *choosing* it, is a more powerful position to take.

What the public didn't know was that Tyler and I had already been talking and texting. Nothing super romantic, really. Just saying hi, and talking about what was happening on the show as we watched it unfold on TV. But the more I watched, the more I'd thought, *Okay, that's* the guy I'm supposed to be with.

Back on July 19, I had called Tyler and told him that I still cared for him.

He said he still cared for me, too. We agreed it would be nice to go for a drink and hang out the next time he was LA.

When I saw Tyler that night, at the end of July, all of those nervous feelings I'd had about him came rushing back again. The spark was still there. Plus, on *The Bachelorette*, he had picked out a ring. He had wanted to ask me to marry him. As I rewatched the episodes, I'd kept wondering, *What if I'd picked him over Jed? Would things have worked out better?*

I had already broken his heart, and I was scared that it was too good to be true that he might be willing to give me another chance. But the two of us agreed that I would ask him, on live TV that night, during the "After the Final Rose" special, if he might want to go out sometime. And he said yes!

Ending the season that way gave everyone, myself included, new hope for a happy ending.

Tyler and I got in touch right after the show. We couldn't really go "out" anywhere, 'cause it would have created a paparazzi frenzy. The ratings that season were high, and there were a lot of people watching our every move, trying to get the scoop on what might happen between us. All I wanted was for things to be low-key. *Private.* So I invited Tyler to come to my place. I had just moved to an apartment in the Valley. I didn't have any furniture except for a bed, a couch, and a TV. But I figured the two of us could hide away from any prying eyes there.

Setting aside the fact that I'd sent him home, we tried to pick up right where we left off. It was a little awkward at first. Our chemistry was still strong, but we didn't sit real close together. We didn't kiss. We just ordered some food and talked and laughed for hours on my couch. It felt so good to talk openly with someone who was there, someone who'd been through the show with me. And I was so honest with him about how I felt, how my parents loved him, why his family felt so right for me, and how my insecurity led me to make the choices I did. He opened up with me about how much it hurt him, and how strong his feelings for me really were. Neither of us had anybody else we could talk to about any of this, so it just felt good to get it out. But there was a line there we didn't cross—until we cracked open a second bottle of wine. We decided to go up on the roof for some air. Tyler put a playlist on his phone.

"I missed you," I said.

"I missed you, too."

We hugged each other, and his body felt warm in the cool LA breeze. I could feel his muscles under his shirt.

"I've hung out with some other girls since we were together on the show," he said. "But I never felt anything like I feel when you and me hug."

We finally gave in.

He kissed me, and I kissed him back, and it felt like a release of all these months of buildup and tension between us. And it was *real* now, because nobody was there but *us*. Truly nobody. We didn't have to think about what this would look like, or what we might want to say about it on camera the next morning, or how it was going to play out on TV, or what the other "suitors" might think about what we were doing.

Tyler told me he wasn't seeing anybody. He knew I wasn't seeing anybody. We talked about our families, and he told me how much his mother loved me. She was so disappointed when I didn't give him the final rose, he said. She even gave me her number over Instagram so I could text her, I told him.

"I bet our mothers would love each other," I added.

He agreed: "We should go spend some time at my place in Florida, and bring your family along so we can all hang out."

"Oh, my gosh. That would be amazing!"

Finally, we were making plans.

Because there was so much interest in the both of us, airlines were sending us offers for free flights and free vacations.

"Should we go?" we wondered. "Should we take one of these offers?"

We talked about taking a *trip* together. Just the two of us.

Tyler stayed the night. We were pretty hot and heavy there for a while, and a part of me was ready to open myself up to him completely. But then he stopped.

He stopped.

"I don't want to do this right now," he said. "I care about you."

He said he wanted to take things slow, and that meant *so much* to me. Even after everything we'd been through, he stopped and respected me, which made me fall for him all the more. We slept together in my bed, and I mean that *all* we did was sleep.

The next morning, we ordered some coffee and breakfast from the market down the street. He walked in to pick it up, and I waited around the corner, just so no one in the place would think we were walking in as a couple. We went back to my apartment, and it seemed like nobody noticed us.

Tyler had to catch a flight to New York City that day. He had some clothes with him, but he didn't even have a proper suitcase. So he borrowed one of mine.

We kissed goodbye, and when I walked him out to his car, the paparazzi were waiting outside my apartment building. I don't know who tipped them off, but as soon as we opened the door, they got pictures. We just knew it would cause all kinds of gossip, but what could we do? We just laughed it off, and I ducked back inside.

That was August 2.

He texted goodbye to me before his flight took off, and he texted me right after he landed. We texted all day the next day, and talked more about our plans to take a vacation together—just the two of us—to get away from everything and just be alone. It all filled me up with so much hope. Maybe going on TV had led me to the man I was supposed to be with after all.

I know I was jumping the gun a little bit, but Tyler and I *connected*. We'd gone through this crazy experience together and come out of it still wanting each other. I had guarded my heart so much with him on the show, and now I was thinking that maybe I should have let those walls come down sooner.

I wasn't delusional. After everything we'd been through, we needed to take it slow. Everything went so fast and it was so messed up, I was ready to take it slow. I needed to take it slow. The idea that we might have a second chance at this felt good, and I didn't want to mess it up.

Then, on August 4, he called me. We talked for a little while, and he told me, "It's so great that we're talking again, but I just want to make sure we're on the same page that we can see other people."

I was like, "Oh. Well, I don't know. I know that we're not exclusively dating, but I know for me, I just dated thirty guys and that didn't work out so well. So I want to focus on seeing if this will work out between you and me. And if it doesn't, it doesn't. But that's where I'm at."

"Okay," he said, "I've gotta go, so can we talk about this later? I'll call you when I'm free."

"Okay," I said, and we said goodbye.

But he never called me back.

I woke up the next morning to find paparazzi photos of Tyler tagged all over Instagram. Tyler, in New York City—on a date with supermodel Gigi Hadid.

Tyler met up with a *supermodel* after getting off the phone with *me*.

This wasn't a TV show. This wasn't some game. My time with Tyler at my apartment wasn't some meaningless hookup, the way it was portrayed in the press. My heart was on the line. And he broke it. With a *supermodel*. Can you imagine? I was so embarrassed, and hurt, and it was all so public. Again. It all caught me so off guard.

And what's crazy is, I loved Gigi Hadid! I thought she was the coolest. I still do. I get it. I would even go on a date with her. I wanna be her friend! But never did I expect to be in a love triangle with her.

I was far too broken to put up with it. I had just been so vulnerable with him. I was so honest about how I felt about him. And then this?

I had to do press the next morning for ABC, and everyone wanted to know what was going on. "I don't *know* what's going on!" is the only thing I could say.

I finally messaged him: "I know why you didn't call me last night, but I'm about to go do press, and I don't know what to say."

He didn't respond. Which meant I had no choice but to go on camera and try to play the role of the strong, independent woman again. I had to play it cool.

When he finally called me, he tried to explain himself, like every guy tries to explain himself, and argue his side of the story. "You got to date thirty guys, so I'm gonna date around and see if I still want to be with you," he said.

"But this isn't a TV show," I said. "You just told me you weren't seeing anybody else. And then you said you wanted to talk about it, but we never talked about it, and like an hour later you went out with her!"

On the show he'd treated me with so much respect. I said, "I hyped you up as this respectful king, and this feels like you're disrespecting me more than anybody ever has in my life! I'm going to be asked about you and Gigi now, constantly. Do you not understand that? I'm the one who has to answer for what you're doing."

I was so mad.

We basically hung up on each other.

I had picked myself up and dusted myself off and tried, again, to be open to love, and got lied to again. And hurt again. By a man who had given me every indication that he wanted to try, too. And it made me feel like I could never trust a man again—just as I was getting ready to start rehearsals for *Dancing with the Stars*.

Now I had even *more* reason to throw myself into this competition with everything I had. I didn't want to *think* about anything else. No men. No heartbreak. Nothing but winning that Mirrorball trophy at the end.

I was laser focused. I was used to having cameras around me now, so much so that I barely even noticed they were there. I met Alan, my dance partner, and I was ready to get down to work.

I had no idea just how much work it was gonna be, and how much it would wreck me, emotionally and physically.

There were times growing up when I went to dance practice right after school until right before bedtime. There were weekends when I felt like all I did was dance.

None of it felt as brutal as the rehearsals for *DWTS*.

In the first two weeks, they wanted us to be there only four hours a day, so we wouldn't wear ourselves out. We were using muscles most of us hadn't used in years, and in some cases, the contestants had never danced before in their lives. We needed to ease into it. But I knew I wanted to stay longer, to learn as much as I could and practice as long as I could. I didn't want to go home to an empty apartment and think again about Tyler, who still hadn't reached out.

Pretty soon, we started rehearsing long hours every day except Sunday. But Sunday wasn't a "day off" for us. We did camera blocking on Sundays for the live shows on Mondays. So we were usually at the studio all day Sunday, too.

Pushing a body to its limits and dancing multiple hours a day is tough. It would be hard enough if I were doing it on my own. But everything I was doing had to be in tandem with my partner, and I had such a hard time with that at first.

Alan kept saying, "You have to trust me if we're going to do this." But trust was the last thing I was prepared to give a man I'd just met.

Ballroom dance and partner dances in general require huge amounts of confidence. With the spins and pulls and lifts, with both of you moving so quickly at times, if you don't know deep down that your partner's got you—I mean *really* got you—either one of you can get seriously physically injured. And when it came to dancing, confident was the last thing I felt. As a child, I had been told repeatedly that I wasn't talented enough to be in the spotlight. I was always put in the back of the group dances. That feeling kept haunting me on *DWTS*. It gave me this paralyzing fear at times, to the point where my feet would freeze up and I wouldn't even be able to try new steps. And there was no time to waste.

It wasn't like we had a lot of time to get it right. After the initial get-to-know-you rehearsals were over, once the live shows started, as the show progressed, we would have to learn two new dances every four days.

By mid-September, I was finally starting to get my footing when someone from *The Bachelor* called and asked me to film some scenes with Peter at the beginning of his season. They asked me if I would consider giving back the pilot's wings he had given to me when we first met, so he could give them to the girl he would now choose to be his "copilot." A girl that wouldn't be me.

It was the very last thing I wanted to do. Emotionally, I was still a mess. After everything that had happened with Tyler, I didn't want anything more to do with that show. But I had no choice. I was still under contract. I couldn't say no.

At the same time, I still had some lingering feelings for Peter. After what happened with Tyler, I couldn't help but think I'd messed this all up. Jed didn't care for me. Tyler didn't really care for me. Peter seemed to be the only guy from the show whose feelings for me were real. And now he was the Bachelor. I didn't want to chase him. I didn't want to go backward. I just wanted to get over it and move on. But because of this new ask from the show, I couldn't help but face my feelings head-on.

I got all dressed up, and they put me into a limousine on his first night, as if I was one of the new girls there vying for his attention. Peter had no idea I was coming. I looked at that mansion, and the sparkling wet pavement, and the crew, and Chris Harrison, and Peter standing there in the spotlight—and I freaked out. I literally had a panic attack. I don't want to make light of this. I'm pretty sure what I felt was some sort of PTSD. I wouldn't get out of the car. I couldn't do it. This was my heart that was at stake. *Peter's* heart, too. I sat in the car for well over an hour. I was a mess.

Finally, I stepped out of the car—and Peter was shocked. At first he thought I was there to be a contestant, and he was actually excited about that. But then I handed him back his pilot's wings, and I encouraged him on his journey, and I left.

I went back home, and ate takeout alone on my couch.

I wished it was the end of it, but rumor had it that they were already talking about bringing me back to the show again. So it stayed there in the back of my mind, the whole time I was in rehearsals and getting ready for the next week's performance on *DWTS*.

Monday, September 23, was one of my best days ever. Two of my best friends, whom I'd lived with in college, flew into LA to help me celebrate my birthday the next day. And Taylor Swift reposted my performance on the show of a Viennese waltz to her song "Lover." Taylor Swift knew who I was!

But this is why we can't have nice things.

On my birthday, September 24, *The Bachelor* called me back to film some more, this time as the "host" of one of Peter's group dates.

When I arrived on set, I learned that the theme of the date was telling old sex stories. As the host, I was expected to talk about how empowering it was to own my sexuality, and to encourage the girls to do the same by sharing intimate stories with a live audience at this theater in LA. I mean, outside of TV, I would never. I'm not an actress. I didn't want to play this version of me, and I got really upset about it. I felt so embarrassed. I got the impression the girls didn't want me there. *I* didn't want to be there. I'm pretty sure Peter felt awkward, too.

"Can I go now?" I said, and I walked off the set to go cry.

Peter followed. He wanted to see if I was okay. I wasn't.

We decided we needed to talk, and we didn't want to do this in front of the other women and the bright lights and the whole crew, so we walked away. A couple of cameras followed us.

While they showed some of our discussion on TV, a lot of it wasn't aired. And a *lot* of it made my heart hurt all over again.

The biggest thing, the one that took my breath away, is that Peter offered to quit the show if I'd take him back. "If you can say without a doubt that you want to be with me, I'll quit the show," he said.

I couldn't say that. I didn't know if I truly wanted to be with him. I didn't want to make a decision that would effect *his* life so deeply in that moment.

"You can't quit, Peter. They've already started shooting."

"I don't care," he told me.

Looking in his eyes, seeing that passion and fight he had for me, I wanted to kiss him. But I couldn't kiss him. The cameras were there. What a mess that would've been! And what would that kiss have meant? Would I have kissed him and then disappeared while he went about dating all those other women who'd just arrived? Would they put me back on the show? I couldn't drop out of *DWTS*. I didn't want to. If he left *The Bachelor* to date me for real, I wouldn't even have time to spend with him. When my parents and my little brother came out to see me on *DWTS*, I barely had time to see *them*.

None of this made any sense, and I wasn't ready to make another big decision. I had to trust my heart there. I had to put an end to it.

"No," I said. "Look, if this doesn't work out for you, I'll still be here. There's no way I'm going to be dating anybody."

I went back to my apartment, ate pizza on the floor with my friends who had flown all the way from Alabama to see me, and cried all over again.

Happy birthday to me.

The next morning, I had to be in rehearsal at 8:00 a.m. to learn the rumba.

It's so hard to be the girl in ballroom dancing. It's harder because it's not just about the strength and the poise and the act of leading; the woman has to do it all in a dress and heels, and backward, and upside down, or standing on one leg. "Balance!" "Hold core!" I had to do a turn while Alan threw me in the air, and keep a smile on my face the whole time. Sure, he had to throw me—and *catch* me. That takes tremendous strength and skill. But I had to do all of that other stuff while looking ladylike and pretty, no matter how twisted up and thrown in the air I might get. So did all the other women. And the pressure to get it right was huge.

Sounds a little bit like a metaphor for old-fashioned male-female relationships, doesn't it? The woman has always had to jump through hoops and twist herself into knots while the man stands there being "strong."

As a dance partner, standing strong, I came to trust Alan more and more every week. I think that showed in our performances. Our chemistry on the stage led to the press speculating that we had something more going on between us, but we didn't. Off the dance floor, we were *not* compatible people.

We performed well together, for sure, but we weren't really compatible in the rehearsal studio, either. We both wanted to win, but our communication styles were just totally different.

I felt like maybe the best way to get through all of the drama was by talking about it. Maybe that could be good, right? Maybe I could channel some of those big feelings on the stage. But after sharing something really personal with Alan, there were times when he would just blow me off. He didn't even ask about my *Bachelor* stuff.

I would tell him everything whether he asked or not, so he could understand why I seemed to be crying for no reason, but he never asked me about any of it himself until a week before the finale, in mid-November, in the context of filming a scene for the show. So it felt like we were on pretty different frequencies.

When the emotional fatigue of the past year caught up with me, I broke down in tears. Anyone who watched my season knows I cried a lot on that show, but I can tell you now it was less about the stress of the dancing than it was about the stress on my heart.

My heart was exhausted.

There are always tears on *Dancing with the Stars*. There are always fights. It's intense work between partners who've only just met. But Alan and I had the most volatile relationship of the season, by far. It was either we acted like best friends and true partners, or we couldn't stand each other. He'd push me too far in rehearsals, and I'd say, "Get out of my face. I'm not doing this," and he'd say, "You're lazy! You're not trying!"

While I worked hard and focused on the prize, and concentrated on becoming a better dancer every day, the process itself kept bringing out the worst in me.

I was emotionally unwell. I was on the brink of tears every day, and nobody on the set knew what to do. On one hand, I was a girl who was living her dream, but then I couldn't stop crying. I would stand up for myself one minute, and then shut back down the next. I was so tired and so lost that I cried in my apartment pretty much every single night. As millions of people watched me on TV, thinking I was doing fine, I was "winning" and "improving" and "being strong," I felt more and more alone.

I didn't reach out for help. I didn't reach out in prayer. I disconnected almost completely from any friends I had. I know now, looking back on it, that was not the right thing to do. I had people in my corner who wanted to help me, who were just waiting for me to call. Maybe if I had called them things would have gotten better sooner.

The only thing that seemed to be getting better for me in those three or four months was my dancing. After always being put in the back line as a kid, I was right out front now in the spotlight. I worked harder and harder every week, getting closer and closer to taking that Mirrorball trophy for myself. It was the only thing that I thought I could look forward to.

I pushed myself hard and put *so* much expectation on myself—an approach that hadn't always been the winning thing for me in the past. But every second I had was focused on winning. Not enjoying it. *Winning.* Because I *needed* that win. When Tom Bergeron and Erin Andrews were busy interviewing other contestants, I kept practicing off to the side. When I got home at night, I watched tapes of myself, like a football player might. I obsessed over every move, every detail, of being the dancer I needed to be to come out on top.

And this time? Focusing on winning *worked.*

My partner and I wowed the judges. We wowed the audience. And we won.

I won the trophy!

The audience cheered, and buckets of confetti poured down from the ceiling, and I felt . . . let down.

I'd spent all this time chasing the high, and once I got it? Once I reached that prize? Well . . . This is what I wrote in my journal a few days later:

I worked to bless myself. I needed to make a win, a positive out of this all. Winning DWTS was my way of doing that. And when I won . . . it felt so empty. I remember standing there waiting for Tom and Erin to answer, almost feeling emotionless. I didn't hear them announce my name as the winner, because I was perplexed by how numb I felt. Why wasn't I excited? I'm standing in the top 2 . . . it felt like I was an onlooker outside of my body like an anxious mom watching her child go to the podium to give a speech and the child just stared blankly to the crowd. That's what I felt like. I was happy for the excitement and celebration Alan was feeling . . . but the feeling I had was "Well . . . I did it. What's next?" I hate admitting this. It shouldn't have been that way. I worked so hard but I was so miserable. Winning and having no feeling and still feeling defeated because the high wasn't all you thought it would be I think is more heartbreaking than losing and feeling the sting of the defeat. And I've felt my fair share of heartbreaking losses, too.

I went to hold up my trophy. The glorious Mirrorball trophy. I prepared for the weight of the shimmering gold-plated trophy to find it . . . weightless. It looked so pompous and grand on the outside, but it was hollow inside. And doesn't that just symbolize the whole experience for me? I'm glistening beautifully as I twirl on the dance floor, but I'm really empty and in a million pieces as I fall from the hollow high.

The trophy literally broke on the way to NYC for our GMA appearance the next morning. The one thing I put everything into amounted to nothing.

I won DWTS, and I have never been less confident.
I still think I can't really really dance.

It was NOT ENOUGH.

I WAS NOT ENOUGH.

It was merely the hardest, most all-
consuming distraction I could find to not deal
with what was going on in my heart.

CHAPTER 20

Heels in My Hands

I suffered a broken toe, bruised ribs, and more on *DWTS*, and I kept telling myself, "Take a cortisone shot. Get through the week, and then when you win, you'll have time to heal!" It was like that in the pageant world, too: "Let's put a Band-Aid on it, let's get through it. You can cry when you get home." Whenever I scraped my knee as a little girl, I'd been taught to just rub some dirt on it and keep going, too.

I had done that all my life.

Pain is what we feel when something isn't right in our bodies. When something is bruised or broken or cut, it hurts, and the pain we feel is letting us know that it needs to be looked at and tended to. It's the same with the pain in life, in your heart, in your mind, in your soul. When you don't take time to rest and tend to the emotional pain you're in, chances are you'll seek out some sort of temporary relief. For some it's drugs or alcohol. For some it's pouring everything into their work. For me it was always "What is the next distraction I can find?" instead of tending to whatever was crying out to be healed.

I needed to stop doing that to my heart. I needed to stop rubbing dirt on my emotional scars. I needed to rest and take whatever time I needed to take. To heal.

The thing is, there are times when you're moving too fast or maybe headed in the wrong direction, when if you don't stop your life, God will stop it for you.

After *DWTS* was over, I finally got a break, and I rested—for like two whole weeks over the holidays.

That wasn't even *close* to what I needed.

I went home to Alabama, and slept in my old bed, and then came back to LA in January 2020 to get ready for my one performance on the *DWTS* tour.

DWTS was such an incredible experience, and I wish I had allowed myself to have more fun with it than I did. But I was in just too much of an emotional state to handle anymore, and certainly not a whole tour. I needed a break. And heck, maybe if they ever do another *DWTS: All-Stars*, they'll invite me back on. Because I sure would love to compete on that show when my heart isn't aching so much.

I used some of my earnings from my time on TV to move into a new apartment. It was still near studios, in a busy part of the city. A lot of people don't know this about Los Angeles, but the Hollywood area can be an hour-plus to drive to the ocean in traffic, and it seems like there's *always* traffic. What I always wanted was to live by the beach. But I thought I needed to be in the center of everything for whatever would come next in my "career." That's where everyone told me I should be. The beach was "too far away," they said. So I listened.

On the positive side, the money I made from *The Bachelorette* allowed me to pay off my student loans and my credit cards. But after spending money on hairstylists and makeup artists and clothes and shoes for my appearances and events outside of the show, it wasn't like I was rolling in dough. The only splurgy thing I bought for myself was a top-of-the line coffee maker: a Jura. I *love* good coffee, and this thing is like having a personal barista on my kitchen counter.

It was also pretty cool to get invited to celebrity-filled parties and red-carpet events. I didn't go to many, but when I did, I usually showed up, said hello to whoever I needed to say hello to, posed for a few photos, and left. I just didn't feel comfortable in that world. What *was* I? I was surrounded by actors and actresses, musicians, designers, directors. I was none of those things. I didn't feel like I really belonged.

Living in LA after disconnecting from friends during *DWTS* was lonely. I spent most nights ordering takeout and eating on my sofa with a plastic fork.

You would think a former Bachelorette and *DWTS* winner who was now single would get all sorts of interesting DMs from guys looking to take her on a date. But that wasn't happening. So every once in a while, I'd respond to a party invite and get all dressed up and go out to have a little fun by myself, just to break out of my loneliness.

Lonely is definitely how I was feeling when Peter called me, just before his season started airing on TV. I hadn't spoken to him since the night he told me he would be willing to leave the show for me.

When he called, he told me all about what had happened on the show, and since I was already sworn to secrecy, he let me know that he and Hannah Ann had gotten engaged. He also told me on that very first call that he was already having doubts.

He said he understood me so much better after going through the experience of being the lead on the show himself. He understood how much pressure I was under, 'cause he felt it, too. In a way, we now had even more in common than we did before.

We stayed in touch as the first few episodes aired—the ones I appeared in—and he confided to me that he and Hannah Ann were having some issues. He also told me he still had feelings for Madison.

Peter would have to keep up a good face for the press for the next couple of months while knowing his engagement might be in trouble. It was crazy. This show was meant to be focused on romance and love, but so many of us who went on it found ourselves caught up in emotional disasters.

I started journaling more, trying to make sense of it all and break some of my unhealthy patterns, but I also was still drinking a bit more than I had before, to numb the pain. And that was definitely the case one night in February when I went to Hannah Godwin and Dylan Barbour's engagement party. Tyler wasn't there, but every other guy from my season of *The Bachelorette* was, including Jed—and his new girlfriend. We avoided each other at first, until I got up the courage to walk right up to him and say hello. I didn't want it to be awkward. He said he was doing good, and I said, "Good. Good for you." And that was about it.

I talked to most of the other guys, too, but the guy I wanted to see most was Peter.

"Hi!" he said. We got to talking, and we just hit it off.

"I have so much to tell you about," he said, but there were producers and other people from the show around. So he couldn't get into it. If we'd spent too much time together, people would've talked.

"I'll just text you later," he said.

"No! I want to know! What's up? I want to know now!"

"We can't talk here," he said. "I have a flight in the morning. I'm about to leave, but I'll text you when I'm in my car. Come out then."

The idea made me feel like I was sneaking out of my parents' house, like a teenager.

Peter left, and then he texted me to come out.

I said my goodbyes, went outside, and hopped in the passenger seat of his car.

He offered to drive me home, so we could just catch up on everything on the way. And in the next few minutes, he told me that he had broken off his engagement to Hannah Ann, he had tried to make amends with Madison, and that after all of that, he and Madison still hadn't worked out. But as he pulled up to my apartment building, we weren't done talking.

"Do you want to just come up?" I asked.

"Well," he said. "I have this flight in the morning. I still have to get my stuff together. Do you want to come to Agoura, we'll keep talking, and then I'll drive you back?"

I didn't want to say goodbye yet, so I said, "Sure."

He took me back to his place, which, if you didn't know from the show, was also his parents' house. He still lived with his parents, in the very same town outside LA as the Bachelor mansion—and his mom was still awake when we got back. We ended up talking, just small talk and stuff, and she told me all about her feelings about the women Peter had brought home during his season. It was so uncomfortable for me . . . and Peter just went upstairs and went to bed and left me there with his mom!

His mom said I should just spend the night, and offered me Peter's brother's room. She was always super nice to me, but it was all so weird.

I crawled into Peter's brother's bed, and a few minutes later, Peter texted me: "Come cuddle."

I lay there in the bed, hitting my head against the pillow, like, "Hannah, what are you gonna do? Don't do it!"

But I did it.

I didn't go there expecting us to have sex. But we did.

I'm not sure what to say about it, except that it wasn't good. I thought we were reconnecting. I was lonely. But it wasn't right. Our connection wasn't the same as it used to be. He wasn't as caring in bed. It was awkward to have to be quiet, knowing his parents were basically down the hall.

The sex didn't last very long, and afterward, we both rolled over and fell asleep.

When he woke me up, he was already dressed in his Delta uniform and getting ready to leave.

"Sleep as long as you want," he said. "My dad's downstairs and looking forward to saying hi to you. I hope you don't mind."

"I . . ."

I was groggy and tired, a little hungover, and so confused.

"Yeah, I guess," I said. "Call me later?"

"All right," he said.

He kissed me on the cheek, he walked out of his bedroom, and he closed the door quietly behind him.

I definitely wasn't going back to sleep after that. I got up right away and put on a pair of Peter's sweatpants and a T-shirt and did the walk of shame into his family kitchen. Carrying my dress over one arm, my high heels dangling from my fingertips, I walked in to find Peter's dad, in a robe, drinking his morning coffee.

"Hello," I said awkwardly.

Peter was still there. "I'm sorry. I have to go," he said. "Can I give you some money for an Uber?"

He handed me a hundred-dollar bill. And I took it.

I was *so* ready to go home.

I stayed and politely talked with Peter's dad until the car showed up, then Uber'd back to my apartment.

✳

I truly didn't think I could feel any worse about myself and my decisions than I did in that private moment, which I've never told anyone about until right now.

Peter texted me that night and thanked me for being there for him, for being so understanding. I told him I thought what we'd done was pretty reckless. And he agreed. "Yeah," he said, "maybe we shouldn't play with that fire again."

He texted some more, and I told him he seemed awful nonchalant about it, like we'd just high-fived or something.

Then he called me and told me about how he was feeling—about *Madison*. It was just the weirdest thing.

I didn't understand why all of this was happening.

I didn't understand why I had made these horrible decisions.

Once again, I felt embarrassed. I was ashamed of my behavior. And once again, I found myself pulling away from my connection to God—just when I needed Him most.

✳

A few nights later, I turned on Peter's latest episode of *The Bachelor*, and I couldn't take it anymore. I sat there bawling in my apartment, with snot running down my face, beating myself up for doing something so stupid, and hating myself for disconnecting from so many of my friends during *Dancing with the Stars*. I felt like I had no one I could call.

But then I remembered the women's conference. I remembered all of those women praying over me at Oasis. And I called a pastor from that church, a friend named Elyse.

I was embarrassed. I thought she might be mad at me for disappearing on her, and I said so.

"No, no, no. I completely understand," she said.

I was so grateful that I started crying.

"Maybe you can come over and watch *The Bachelor* with me?" I said.

She paused for a second, and then she laughed. It made me laugh, too—right through my tears. I grabbed a tissue and wiped my eyes and my nose.

"I would love that, Hannah," she said. "Whatever you need."

Elyse started coming to watch *The Bachelor* with me every week, and it made it less sad for me and more fun. We talked, and we laughed about what was happening, and one night, right after the show ended, I asked her, "Can I tell you something?"

"Of course," she said.

"I feel very distant from the Lord."

Elyse looked at me and nodded, like she knew this was coming.

She grabbed the remote and turned off the TV.

"I feel Him calling on my heart," I said, "but I've shut Him out so much."

"Why?"

My eyes welled up with tears.

"Because I know He's going to break my heart because of all of this stuff that's been happening. There's a lot of hurt, and I'm not ready to surrender it," I said.

Elyse gave me a great big hug and said, "Babe, all you've got to do is pray. Just surrender to it. Ask for forgiveness. It's okay. It's okay to do that."

We sat in my apartment, and she helped me let go. She helped me pray, and it was one of the hardest things I've ever had to do—because I felt ashamed for not doing it in the first place.

I just couldn't seem to get started on my own.

"What do you want?" she asked.

"Freedom from all of this," I replied.

I don't even know where those words came from, but I meant them. I needed freedom—from all of the pressure, the hurt, maybe even from the spotlight I'd been in for the last year.

"Let's pray for that," she said. "Freedom. From all of this."

"Yes," I said.

"Say, 'God, I'm back!'"

I took a deep breath and shouted right out loud, "God, I'm back!" and we both started laughing. It just felt good.

"Lord, it's hard for a Christian girl to admit this," I prayed, "but in my heart, I feel I have let you down. I've been trying to do everything myself, and I haven't talked to you in so long . . ." The more I spoke, the more I prayed, the more I felt the weight lift off my shoulders.

When you allow the Lord to take everything, there's a feeling of no shame or guilt. The grace is so overpowering. It feels so good, but it's also scary to release like that.

I know this doesn't all make sense to some people. But it made such a difference to me.

Praying allowed me to start to breathe again; to release some of the guilt and shame I felt, and the hurt I felt, and to know that God was there for me, just listening and watching over me—just like when I was a little girl, so sure of my faith without even trying. That prayer immediately made things better. It was just that easy. I almost laughed at myself, like, why had I been letting myself be so miserable?

I knew why: it's because I felt unworthy.

What I discovered, once again, is that when you've lost your connection to God, all you have to do is start again. Say, "Hey. I'm back."

Wake up in the morning, say a prayer, meditate, do your devotion, read a passage from the Bible—whatever is best for you. Because He never left, and all God wants is for you to spend time with Him. You don't have to feel that you're not worthy of that. You never have to feel that you're not worthy of that. You don't have to be perfect! You don't have to be anything but you, exactly as you are.

The reason I told myself I didn't have time for the Lord was that I was scared of what I would hear if I actually started listening. What would He do if I gave him all control? *Can I really handle that right now?* I thought. *I'm barely holding on as it is.*

But I'm pretty sure now that the *reason* I was barely holding on was that I wasn't making time for *Him*.

CHAPTER 21

Everything Changes

I had always struggled with being content.

That February of 2020, I actually looked up the definition of the word: "Contentment is the state of being mentally or emotionally satisfied with things the way they are."

Oh, I thought. *Contentment is a* good *thing!*

For years I'd suffered an irrational fear of contentment, in part because I saw it as complacency—and they are *not* the same thing. Being complacent is just allowing things to be as they are, even if you don't agree with them or even if they're hurting you. That's not a good thing. But I thought of contentment as just accepting the status quo, too, as if being content meant I was being lazy. I suppose that's an easy conclusion to make in this society, which constantly tells us all to "Go, go, go!" and "Do, do, do!" But the going and doing and worrying about what's next can leave you with a lot of anxiety.

After that night with Elyse, I was finally starting to feel some contentment. And let me tell you, for someone like me, who was always worried and anxious, it felt good to be even a little bit content. I was surrendering the worry and asking God to direct my life. I was taking little steps every day. I was getting a routine back, focused on spending time in prayer.

I had also started working out every day. Not for a competition or a show, but for *me*. I took up boxing. Sometimes I would be in the middle of a workout and my trainer would yell, "Breathe! Remember to breathe!" I literally would stop breathing while punching the bag. I didn't even know I was doing it.

In life I realized I'd been holding my breath, too. I had to learn what it feels like to take a long breath instead of just short little ones to get me through my days, and that would take training, too.

As part of that training, I consciously decided not to rush into whatever the next thing was that came my way, whether it was a new TV offer or getting asked on a date by some man. I wanted to take my time deciding what I wanted to do next with my life, and I kept praying for that. For time. For patience. For freedom.

Preparing my own mind and body for whatever was next sure felt better than worrying about it, or forcing it, or just jumping into things that I wasn't prepared to handle. I guess I probably should have known that already, but I didn't.

When I was growing up, there was a framed verse from the Bible on my bedroom wall:

> *Do not worry about tomorrow, for tomorrow will take care*
> *of itself.*
>
> —MATTHEW 6:34

Worrying about what might happen next never helped me, because life is never fully in our control, no matter how hard we try to control it. All we can do is try to do our best, and prepare ourselves to be strong and resilient when something happens that we aren't expecting.

If 2020 taught me anything—if 2020 taught us *all* anything—it's that everything can change.

In an instant, everything can change.

*

On Monday, February 24, Tyler's mom, Miss Andrea, sent me a message on Instagram. It was a fan video of a clip from an old interview with Tyler, one in which he said that I was even prettier in person than he'd expected me to be.

She was always sending me things like that.

"Aw, that's sweet," I responded.

"Yes, it was," she wrote back. "I know it made me smile."

She and I had exchanged messages every once in a while, and sometimes it was hard for me, because Tyler and I still weren't talking to each other. She wished that we would get back together, and she wasn't shy about saying it. I can't say I wished the same thing. But I still cared about him. And Miss Andrea was so sweet and kind, I was glad she was still in my life.

Three days later, Tyler wrote on Twitter that he was canceling all of his upcoming appearances—and he asked everyone to please pray for his mom.

The message was vague, and we hadn't spoken to each other at all, but I felt like I should reach out to him. So I did. I texted him. I said I'd seen his tweet, and I was thinking about him, and "just praying that everything's okay."

He answered right back. "Thank you so much," he wrote. "She loved you."

He kept talking about his mom in the past tense. Then he told me, "She had a brain aneurysm. I'm here with her now, holding her hand, and I was just thinking about how much she loved you—and you just texted me."

I couldn't believe it. It was shocking, and just so sad.

Then Tyler thanked me again for reaching out. "I would love to be able to talk one day and put all this stuff behind us," he said.

"I'm here if you want to talk," I responded.

Later that day he ended up calling me, and we talked about everything. He told me Miss Andrea was on a ventilator, but she wasn't really alive anymore. They were keeping her alive. She was only fifty-five years old. Tyler's voice sounded so lost.

During that call, he apologized for how he'd handled everything with me, and it just felt good to feel like we could put it all behind us. When something like that happens, you just do. Tyler and I had shared so much in a very short time. Setting everything else aside, we had been open with each other about our families, and some really deep stuff. I told him again that I was there for him, and I texted to check on him the next day, when I drove out to Malibu to celebrate a friend's baby shower.

In all the time I'd spent in LA, it was only the second time I'd been out to that seaside town, and just knowing I was headed to the beach made me smile.

I was still thinking about Miss Andrea, and about Tyler, but I had spent a good part of that month trying to get myself centered, and the beach was the perfect place for me to get back to trying to do that.

It was a beautiful day spent hanging out with girlfriends, watching the sun go down over the Pacific as the sky turned all sorts of amazing colors. And I went to sleep to the smell of the salt air, and completely forgot to plug my phone in before I went to bed.

I picked it up when I woke up, and was staring at a blank screen. I borrowed a cord and let it charge, and as soon as it turned on I saw five missed calls from my mom, along with a bunch of text messages: "CALL ME."

I called her right away.

"Oh, thank God," she said when she picked up the phone.

"What is wrong?" I asked.

"It's Patrick. He overdosed last night. He's in the hospital."

"What? Is he okay?"

"No," she said. "He's on a ventilator. Please come home, Hannah. He needs you."

My relationship with my brother had always been strained, and for the last couple of years, it was clear that he'd been running with a rough crowd. He'd been drinking. He'd done all kinds of drugs, both uppers and downers, and my parents didn't seem to be able to do anything to stop him.

While I'd been struggling with all of these matters of the heart and trying to come to grips with the mistakes I'd made, he'd been struggling in a whole different way—acting out and causing my parents all kinds of stress, like he'd always done, ever since he was a little kid. And I'll be honest: my first reaction when my mom told me the news was anger.

I hung up the phone and walked down by the water, and I sat on a rock, and I didn't cry, and I didn't scream . . . I just sat there thinking, *This cannot be happening.*

I couldn't get a flight home that day. Everything was booked. While I was trying to figure out how I could get home, Tyler let me know that his mom had passed away the night before, too. They took her off the ventilator. She was gone. Miss Andrea, who was so warm and welcoming to me that she made me think I could fit right into

Tyler's life, was *gone*. Tyler's *mom* was gone. It just broke my heart. I told him how sorry I was.

I also let Tyler know that my brother had overdosed, and that he was on a ventilator, and he told me how sorry he was for me.

He told me they were going to plan some sort of a celebration of life for Miss Andrea. "I think she would have wanted you to come," he said.

"Of course I'll come. I want to be there," I responded. "Just let me know when."

He texted later that day to say he was thinking of me, which I thought was so sweet and unexpected when he already had so much to deal with on his own.

We were both going through these nightmares at the same time, and we seemed to be able to lean on each other. The weight of what was happening was just so much more important than any of the problems we'd had. Our hearts rose above the mess of it all when it mattered most.

I flew home the next morning, March 2, with nothing but some sweats and whatever else I could fit into the overnight bag I had brought with me to Malibu.

I didn't think I'd be in Alabama for more than a few days.

When I arrived at the hospital, my parents told me the doctors were just taking Patrick off the ventilator. At first I thought that meant the worst, but what they meant was he was breathing on his own. He was awake. He was gonna make it—and *that*, they said, was a miracle.

Patrick had apparently ingested an opioid that was laced with three times the lethal dose of fentanyl. He didn't know it was laced with fentanyl at all.

When I first got there, I was still angry at him. But when I walked into his room and saw him in that hospital bed, the anger was replaced by something else. I felt numb in some ways, like I just couldn't believe it.

It looked like he was almost embarrassed to see me; as if I was the mom and he was scared about what I might say. And I might have acted that way toward him in the past. But as he lay there, looking so broken, it hit me: I was just so glad that he was *alive*. I didn't want him to be scared of me. This wasn't the time to lecture him.

"I'm so glad you're okay," I said.

I told him I loved him. And I prayed with him.

It was only later on that I said to him, "So . . . what's next? I mean, things have got to change after this, right?"

Thankfully, Patrick agreed.

He embraced the idea of going into rehab, which was a requirement for him to leave the hospital. And because he was serious about it, I did some research and asked some friends and found him a really strong in-patient program down in Texas. He never could have afforded it himself, and I don't think my parents could have afforded it in that moment, either. Thankfully, because I had made some money from going on TV, I was able to wire the large deposit they needed to secure him a spot.

They say the Lord works in mysterious ways. In that moment, everything I had been through, all the pain and embarrassment and shaming I'd endured, somehow seemed worth it.

Patrick developed pneumonia in the hospital and had to wait a few days for his lungs to get better before traveling to Texas.

That's when Tyler called me and asked me to come down to his mother's celebration of life in Jupiter, Florida.

I was planning to stay at a hotel, but Tyler made the effort to find me a guesthouse where I could stay with one of his friends. He introduced me to all of his friends, too. I was there to support him, but he wanted to spend so much time with me. I only stayed a couple of days, but we spent most of those days and nights together. He cried with me about his mom. *Wow,* I thought. *I still really care about this person.*

I came back home to be with my brother before he went into rehab, and a few days later we managed to get him settled in Texas—just as the whole country started shutting down because of the pandemic. COVID-19 had not only arrived in America, it was spreading like wildfire, including in Los Angeles. I wasn't sure if that city was the safest place for me to go back to. Everything felt so uncertain.

Tyler had to go to New York on some business, but since COVID was bad in New York, he turned right around and went back to Jupiter.

That was right when the government was starting to tell people to stay put and quarantine—when everyone assumed that it wouldn't last for more than a couple of *weeks*—and Tyler asked me if I wanted to come quarantine in Jupiter with him and his crew.

He had talked to some of his friends about it, he said, and they told him that this could be a perfect time for the two of us to "figure it out," as he liked to say. "When else will we have a chance to just hang out like this?"

I had no concrete reason to go back to LA. I had some potential sponsorships lined up, and some meetings I was supposed to take, but it was nothing that had to be done in-person. I could call in to meetings and take photos just about anywhere. So I said, "Why not?"

A lot of businesses and offices were closing down in LA, and if I had to quarantine for a few days anyway, Jupiter, Florida, with Tyler and his friends seemed like a perfect place for me to be.

Only it wasn't just for a few days. Once I flew down there, I found out that we weren't supposed to leave. The COVID-19 travel restrictions set in, and I wound up staying there nearly a month.

The fact that the two of us were spotted together in Jupiter drew all kinds of attention from social media. My Instagram audience blew up, which really surprised me, since I wasn't on TV anymore. Tyler's audience grew, too. So we toyed with it. We started filming ourselves and putting up silly TikTok dances and Insta posts with our whole "Quarantine Crew," and the media went nuts for it.

Suddenly there was all this pressure. The world wanted to know if we were dating. (I wanted to know that, too!)

I told Tyler I still had feelings for him, and he said he had feelings for me. But then everything kept happening so quickly. We were drawing so much interest on social media that some powerful people in New York and LA started asking us if we wanted to work together. For a hot minute, the two of us wondered if we should try to do some sort of a TV show.

Tyler was into construction. I loved interior decorating. We thought maybe we could team up, like Chip and Joanna Gaines! We talked briefly about making plans, and what we were going to do when the pandemic was over, when things got back to normal.

Things weren't normal, though.

Neither one of us had taken the time to rest, to grieve, to heal from the wounds we'd suffered, and the loves and lives we'd lost.

Two unhealthy people do not make for a healthy relationship. Not even a "friendship," or whatever it was we had. We slept in the same bed for twenty days, and he never tried to kiss me or anything. I started to wonder if there was something wrong with me. Like, "Is it because he sees me in the morning without makeup on?" I started to get so self-conscious. It was honestly miserable.

After a while, he started treating me like I was just annoying. Like he didn't want me around. Some days, he wouldn't even talk to me.

That's when his friend Matt James and I started really talking, and he and I had more in common than me and Tyler. "What is going on?" I asked him. "Am I doing something wrong?"

"Hannah," Matt said, "you're not doing anything wrong. It's just very obvious that he is trying to distract himself from everything."

I knew what he meant by that. I'd done plenty of distracting myself.

There were moments when it felt like Tyler and I were going to be more than friends. On some nights, we cuddled, and he would say things like, "You obviously still care for me, and I still care for you. Let's figure this out." And then he wouldn't talk to me the whole next day.

He tried to tell me that he just didn't want to talk about what this relationship was, or what was happening. And that wasn't what I wanted to talk about, either. At one point, I said, "I don't care what we talk about. We can talk about football! I just want you to talk to me."

His mom had just died, so it's hard for me to criticize how he was acting. I know he was hurting. But I was stuck there. I couldn't leave. And it felt terrible.

When I finally figured out a way to get back to Alabama, Tyler gave me a side hug, and then we didn't talk the rest of the day. He texted to make sure I got home, and then I didn't hear from him for another week—after I'd just lived with him and slept in his bed for twenty days.

The whole thing just got so weird. We tried to remain friends after that. Many months later, Tyler came out to LA and we filmed a YouTube video together, talking about our relationship and the mistakes we'd made. I was hopeful that we'd be able to hang out and sort of rebuild the friendship, and for him to meet my friends since I'd met all of his, but it always seemed like he had other plans. Or that our plans weren't his priority. I felt sort of embarrassed, and like I'd misunderstood what was going on.

I had to get honest with myself: even though I saw the good in him, my relationship with Tyler was not good for me. I realized we were on two different paths, and while I supported him on his, I wasn't gonna do it at the cost of mine.

No matter how much we talked, and connected, I always felt like his bench girl. Like I was the backup player who never got to play in the game. I was the girl he would confide in. He told me I was the only girl he could talk to for hours and hours on the phone. But my vulnerability and availability seemed to get used only when it was convenient for him, in between me watching him go out with other girls in public. And being in that position left me hurting.

The thing I know now that I wish I'd known then was that if someone really likes you, if they love you, you'll know. And if they don't? You'll feel confused.

A relationship that's right shouldn't be so hard. Sure there might be some things to work out, and some tough stuff you deal with. But overall? I deserve to be in a relationship that feels easy. Easy and good. Not hard and dramatic.

Tyler took up way too much space in my head, and lived there rent free for way too long.

I eventually told him I couldn't really be friends with him anymore. "It just hurts me too much," I said. "I just need some space. Maybe down the line we can try it again."

That happened about six months before I sat down to write this page in my book—and I haven't heard from him since.

His last poetic words to me were, "Well . . . if you rock with me, you rock with me. If you don't, you don't."

I wish I was making that up.

I gave up my apartment in LA. I had only signed a short-term lease, and it didn't make sense to pay for a place when I wasn't living there full-time, especially when nobody knew how long this pandemic might last.

As a result, the rest of my quarantine time was spent stuck in Alabama, where the only "crew" I had was my family. I realize everyone was cooped up while quarantining. I'm not alone in this. But the pandemic was really messing with people's heads, and it was definitely messing with mine. I locked myself in my childhood bedroom as my safe place, and I shut off almost all real communication with friends in the outside world.

I also stopped praying. Not for any particular reason. I just stopped.

It wasn't long before I fell right back into the sad, awful place I was in when I came home from *Dancing with the Stars*—only this time, I had new scars from Peter and Tyler etched deep into my heart, and the trauma of nearly losing my brother weighing on my soul.

Hollywood shut down. My "career" was suddenly on hold. My stomach churned with worry about what I was going to do next, and where I was going to live. It felt like everything was closing in on me.

I had been in the constant spotlight now for two years, sharing some of my most intimate and personal parts of my life with perfect strangers, and then watching and reading how many "likes" I got and all the comments they left for me.

After Tyler and I stopped streaming and TikToking together, it seemed like the spotlight had turned off—and I wasn't ready for that. So I turned to Instagram Live.

My spotlight now came in the form of the light from the little flash on my iPhone.

Honestly, I think I started going on Instagram Live in order to fulfill whatever needs for connection (or, more likely, validation) I craved for the day. Social media is nothing if it isn't a great substitute for actual relationships. I was just so lonely and miserable in Tusca-loosa. But I didn't want to talk to anyone about what I was feeling. Not even God. So instead I decided to talk to thousands of strangers about nonsense online.

And it really was nonsense.

One time, ten thousand people joined in just to watch me jump rope.

The week of May 11 was always a tough one for me, and for every-one in my family. In case the date doesn't ring a bell for you, that's the week when my aunt and cousins were murdered all those years ago. And now it was also the one-year anniversary of me thinking I was changing my life for the better by adding someone to it: Jed, the man I said yes to in front of the whole world—a day that very quickly left me sitting similarly all alone, feeling empty and completely unsure of what might happen to me next.

I needed to get out of the house. I felt like a change of scenery would help make everyone feel better. And when I found out that you could still rent a beach house on the Alabama coast, I quickly decided to book us all a vacation. I rented a house right on the sand, and my family and I drove down there for a little escape.

I've never been a big drinker (though I love good wine), but at that point I'd say I was escaping my own nagging thoughts and feelings in the way only a nice bottle of wine can provide. Since breaking up with Jed, I'd been drinking more. Sometimes a lot more. It was another way of avoiding the big problems, I guess.

That week, I quickly formed a habit of drinking one, two, usually three glasses at night. I was at the beach. No one was driving anywhere. I was full of pent-up emotions that I hadn't allowed myself to fully process, but since I didn't drink much until the late afternoon, it all felt pretty okay and normal.

Until this one day: May 16, 2020.

I started drinking at 11:00 a.m.—and never really stopped.

While on my Instagram Live that night, I drunkenly read a comment asking me to do a TikTok dance. In the moment, I couldn't think of any that I knew, except for *kinda* knowing the dance to "Rockstar." So I put the music on and tried to remember the dance and the lyrics, all in real time. On IG Live. With thousands and thousands of people watching.

That's when I mindlessly and ignorantly recited a word in the lyrics that should have never come out of my mouth: I sang the N-word.

If you had asked me when I was sober, I would have told you that *of course* saying the N-word is wrong and not in my vocabulary. A white person should never say it, under any circumstances, even when singing along and it's right there in the lyrics. But on that night, I was so drunk that I truly didn't know I said it. When I saw a few comments pop up like, "Did she really just say that?" I had no idea what people were talking about.

Then a whole bunch of comments came flooding in, saying that they heard me say it, and I reacted very defensively. "I would never say that word!" I yelled into my streaming iPhone camera, and then I went into a state of total drunken, nervous embarrassment. I tried to defend my drunken honor.

It was only after I woke up the next morning that I truly realized what I'd done.

I didn't have a couple of DMs. I had *lots* of DMs.

I really *had* said the N-word. And the harsh reality of how much it was blowing up online was like getting a big bucket of ice dumped on me to sober me up. It wasn't just in my comments. This thing went viral. The news media picked it up. I woke to messages on my phone from my agents, my attorney, my friends . . . What had I just done? It was like I woke up in a stranger's bed and didn't know how I got there, or what had happened. None of it made any sense to me.

It was so out of character, and so very wrong—all *kinds* of wrong.

I felt sick. I started crying uncontrollably. I wanted to apologize to everyone and talk about it, but I also knew that I had stepped into something that was much bigger than I knew how to handle. Plus, I was in no shape to talk. I needed to fully understand what I'd done, the repercussions of it. I went to my room and turned off all the lights and played a prayer in my headphones. A calming prayer.

I wanted to address it, and I considered going on Instagram Live and talking about it right away, but I decided I needed to wait a beat. I needed to gain some composure and understanding before opening my mouth again in public. I felt so terrible that I had done something so wrong, and because of who I am, I was filled with shame. I felt like I was "bad," like I wasn't a good person anymore. I for sure didn't want to go on air crying, as a white girl, as if what I was now going through was anything compared to the racism that so many people endure every day of their lives.

I was a public figure by then. That's a lot of responsibility, and a lot of weight to carry. But I chose this, I have benefited from it, and at that point I couldn't walk away from any of it.

No excuses.

I realized I have a responsibility to step into the position that I am in with more awareness, more insight, more compassion, and more knowledge. And that's not just because I'm a public figure. This same thing applies to *anyone*. It's just a part of growing up, and maturing, and accepting that you can't use your upbringing or privilege or old-fashioned ignorance as an excuse anymore.

The blowback from that one moment on Instagram cost me all of my endorsement deals (which was my only source of income) and so much more. It was beyond upsetting to be canceled by people who don't know me. I cried my eyes out for days on end. But I was also humbled by the education that resulted from that moment, which may have never happened had I not gone through this very public lesson in accountability.

In the days following the Instagram Live video, I wanted to speak out and apologize but I felt completely overwhelmed. So many people from my personal and professional life were giving me advice, but I knew I didn't just want to hire a "fixer" or wait for it to blow over. Instead, I sought out someone who could help educate me on what I had done, and who I had harmed. I hired an ethnic studies professor to help me through it all. She led me through an extensive personalized training where we delved deep into my family history, the ideologies that shaped me, and specifically the history of race, racism, and white privilege in the United States.

For a couple of weeks, between three and eight hours a day, the professor pushed and engaged me on these difficult topics I had avoided most of my life. It was a crash course on a history I had never been exposed to before, with someone who had the expertise to explain where many of my emotions and, honestly, ignorance originated. Not knowing this history didn't mean I was racist or dumb, but rather that I was a product of an education system and culture that doesn't teach this history. It wasn't an excuse but rather an invitation to begin my learning, and I threw myself into the process. I invested in my education and it was a great way get out of my head and address the anxiety that was swirling around me at the time. I learned how to identify my own "white fragility" when I was confronted with being called a racist for the first time in my life; ultimately getting pushed and encouraged to open up to her and others in candid conversations.

I was ultimately inspired by how many people supported my learning, and my commitment to growth, from friends and acquaintances to perfect strangers, on Instagram and even in person when I dared to go get a coffee or something.

I didn't feel as if I could have conversations about race before it happened. That's just not something a southern Christian white girl from Alabama has any place or practice doing. But now? It's not even a "could" thing. It's a "should" thing.

I'm trying to focus on that, and not let this moment go away. Some people told me to not even talk about it in this book, but I don't *want* it to be brushed under the rug. It, ironically, has given me the opportunity to share what I have learned with other people, many like me who have never gone deep on these topics. For these reasons and more, I don't want to erase it from my story. I have chosen not to speak about it as much on social media because honestly, I feel such anxiety around how that played out in the past. But here, where I can give more context and share more of my journey, I feel drawn to share what I have been working through.

Before this happened, I wasn't oblivious to the big events or movements around racism, but I certainly didn't think about myself as part of the problem. I know better now.

The only way for me to be better is to *do* better. To work to be part of the solution. To raise my voice and to help others learn from the mistake I made, which I own, and for which I am very, very sorry.

I promise to try to do better for the rest of my life.

To be better and do better—that's progress. It might not be as much as we want or need. But progress is a good thing. Always.

CHAPTER 22

Day By Day

For the rest of 2020 I was stuck in Alabama, cooped up in my room, trying to sort out so much while the virus was spreading everywhere. Half the world was shut down and wearing masks in public.

I needed to get out. So one day I decided to take a walk.

Whenever I left my parents' house, I always walked in the same direction; and every time, a dog in one of the neighbors' yards would run up and bark at me and scare me half to death. It drove me nuts.

On this particular day, I didn't want to deal with the barking. So I left the house and when I got to the road, I turned and walked in the other direction. I realized I had never walked in that direction in my entire life. I don't know why. But I walked under the power lines, and down the hill, and I noticed a dirt road, and I took it.

In a matter of minutes, I was standing there looking out at a beautiful lake.

I had known the lake wasn't all that far away, but we couldn't reach it by car from our property; we always drove there from another spot in town. So it seemed way farther away than it actually was.

My whole life, I had been within walking distance of this lake, and I never even knew it. I stood there in absolute shock. All I had to do to get to the water, in all this time, was turn left instead of right. I had missed out on that peaceful spot, which could have been a perfect getaway, a place to sit and think when I was growing up, maybe even to take a swim in the summer—and it was right there the whole time.

It was a huge lesson for me; a lesson I wanted to apply to everything in my life. I needed to stop doing things the way I'd always done them. I needed to stop repeating my mistakes. I needed to open my eyes to the beauty that was right there in front of me, and I needed to pay attention to what God was trying to tell me.

That barking dog? Maybe it wasn't just annoying. Maybe it was trying to tell me I was going the wrong way!

There were a lot of barking dogs in my life. I either ignored them and walked right by, or petted them and tried to love them. Either way, I wasn't really paying attention to what their barks were trying to tell me.

What if there were a lot of peaceful lakes in my life? Right down the street? And I'd been missing out on them because I kept going the wrong way?

It made me want to reassess every decision I'd ever made. If I wanted to change direction, I needed to look back at my own experiences. I needed to learn from my own life—to learn what worked and what didn't, and how to do better and feel better by learning from both of those things.

As Taylor Swift sings in "New Romantics": "Life is just a classroom."

My life had absolutely been a classroom. And the last two years of it had been like some kind of intensive training program. The only problem was that I got thrown into it so fast. I felt like I'd skipped a grade or two, and there was no teacher at the head of the classroom. I didn't have a copy of the syllabus. I didn't know what was expected of me, and I didn't know what to expect. Now? I felt this overwhelming desire to figure it all out. To do better. To be *happier*. And I just couldn't do it on my own.

I had God. He was with me. He was guiding me. He would not let me down. I knew that. But to find what was missing in my life, I had to listen. And during the pandemic, the message I kept getting was "Go get help." So finally, I listened to my inner voice.

It's interesting. I was taught early on that if you have God in your life, you don't need medicine, you don't need therapy—God will provide all healing. Now, as a full-grown independent-thinking adult, I actually think that's wrong. I don't think all of God's healing happens magically and miraculously in some flash out of the sky. I think He's capable of that, sure. But most of the time, the gift God gives us is the doctors and therapists that He put on this earth who have the talents and skills to make us better. I benefited from the gift of medicine when it came to my anxiety and depression. I couldn't have finished college without it. And now, the overwhelming message I received from God was to talk to someone trained to help heal people's hearts and minds.

At twenty-five years old, I went out and found myself a therapist. I did it all on my own. I didn't wait for my parents or doctors or anyone else to tell me to how to do it, or to give me permission. So what if my parents didn't believe in therapy? It's my life! I took responsibility for my own life, and my own pain, and decided to try to heal it, not ignore it. Not put a Band-Aid on it. Not rub dirt on it and keep going. To actually get to the bottom of it all and *heal*.

I didn't have to look very far. I had met a therapist when I was in Florida, the mother of a friend that Tyler grew up with. They didn't know each other well, and I didn't know her well, but I liked the fact that she already knew a little bit about me. That gave me a head start, which I felt I needed.

The two of us were able to meet remotely by Zoom or FaceTime during the ongoing quarantine. I told her *everything*. She helped me to see my life from perspectives outside of my own narrow views. She helped me to make sense of the stories you've read here, and to allow myself to feel, and to grieve, and to deal with my own emotions, so I could finally move forward instead of staying stuck in the mud.

"Ugh, why has my life been such a mess!" I asked her one day.

"Everyone's life is messy," she said. "Nobody has it easy. The only difference is how you process it."

That was such a revelation to me.

For me, having a therapist has made all the difference in the world. For somebody else, a teacher, a life coach, a mentor, a priest might have been what was needed to help them. But for me, a therapist was the right answer.

You know what else helped? Reading. I started reading self-help books, and Christian books, and rereading my Bible and all my old journals—all in an effort to process it all.

I woke up and did a devotional every day. I prayed. I journaled as much as possible. I made a routine that was right for me. And guess what? I started to feel better.

When you feel better, you can see clearer.

When you see clearer, you make better decisions.

Better decisions build confidence.

Confidence creates a new foundation.

And a strong foundation gives you strength to build on.

The self-help books, the Christian books, the therapy—all of it helped.

But do you know where my biggest revelations came from? They came from *me*.

All I needed to do was get a little help to make sense of the lessons life had been trying to teach me—and which God had been trying to teach me, too.

For example: because of my experiences with men, I had some serious trust issues. That didn't mean I could never trust again. It meant that I needed to learn. It meant that I needed to recognize that from those experiences, I could learn what to look for in men, and how to better discern who was trustworthy and who was not. That is a *huge* lesson in life. That is a gift! I was beating myself up for the longest time over picking the wrong men, thinking I was such an idiot. I *wasn't* an idiot, but I wasn't paying attention to the right things. I was supposed to be learning from those experiences, but I kept ignoring the lessons.

Everything was like that. Everything I had done or not done held a lesson.

And the biggest lesson was to realize the peace I could feel not only by going back to God and by spending time in prayer, but by listening to my inner voice. My whole life I had heard this inner voice, nagging at me, screaming at me at times: "Listen to me! Trust me!" But because I spent so much of my life thinking I wasn't "good enough," I thought that voice inside of me wasn't "good enough," either. So I let other people's thoughts, opinions, and feelings guide me, rather than following my own instincts.

What I didn't realize was that my inner voice was bigger than all of that. That voice, that gut instinct, that thing you're feeling when you sense that something's wrong, or that maybe some guy isn't telling you the truth—that's God. It's the voice of God trying to help you.

I recognized that voice when I broke up with Brady after church one day. So why didn't I recognize it all those other times?

For years I let people tell me, "Quit overthinking," or, "You're being so dramatic," and I listened to *them*—because I didn't believe in *me*. I'm not going to do that anymore. I know now that my inner voice matters. If I had listened to it all along, maybe I could have avoided a lot of pain and suffering. And if I listen to it going forward, maybe life will get a little easier.

Once I was feeling a little better, and seeing a little clearer, I realized it wasn't healthy for me to stay in Alabama any longer. Even though the pandemic was still going on, I knew that I wanted to move back to LA. Not to an apartment in the center of everything, but to an apartment by the ocean.

I didn't have the money for a true oceanfront spot in that crazy-expensive stretch of Southern California, but I *was* able to find a really nice place just a few blocks back from the shore. I can walk on the sand, take a run on the walkway that stretches up and down the coastline, and dip my toes in the Pacific anytime I want to. Every day I get to enjoy the LA sunshine as it sparkles on the water and waves. And at sunset, when I'm sitting on the sand, watching the sky turn pink, I feel good about making that decision, and for trusting myself to make it.

I am exactly where I want to be, doing the work I want to do. Not necessarily the work that other people want me to do (for once), but the good work that needs doing: I'm trying to figure out who I am, and I'm sharing that process with the world—on my YouTube channel, on Instagram, and now through the pages of this book.

If life is just a classroom, then the mess of my own life was the greatest classroom ever—for *me*.

My hope in sharing all of this is that it's serving as a classroom for you, too. Maybe you can learn from my experience and skip over some of the heartbreak. Maybe reading my story will help you to make sense of some of your own life without having to endure what I've endured. It definitely doesn't take years full of pageants and television shows to teach us how to live our lives. Everyone goes through stuff, and everyone can learn from their own experience if they want to. We all just need to learn to embrace our true selves, and maybe to be open and share our experiences with each other—the good, the bad, and the ugly—so we can just do *life* better.

One of the biggest lessons I've learned in all of my slowing down is that the only way to be better rather than bitter is to extend the same grace to others that God extends to us. Which is why today I'm doing my best to forgive everyone who hurt me—and asking for their forgiveness, too.

CHAPTER 23

New Beginnings

I continued my therapy after moving to LA full-time.

One day my therapist asked me to dig deep into my past, and to open up about something I hadn't been able to talk about before then.

I wrote in my journal:

I was talking to my therapist this week and she gave me a task, or an "encouraging nudge," to journal about something I've been terrified to do. I guess today is the day. Not because I want to, but I've realized I can't move forward and continue to write this book if I don't continue to explore this scar that was slit back open this week. We were going through my family history, my relationship with my mom and my dad, how we communicate (or how *we don't communicate), and some defining moments of my childhood naturally began to pour out.*

Including this one . . .

The idea of writing down what happened to my aunt and cousins was terrifying to me. Writing it down felt like I was making it real. Permanent. But I knew I needed to do it.

I had stuffed so many of those memories down and never talked about them, I wasn't even sure what to write. I couldn't remember at first whether my father was home when he told me he couldn't come to my recital. Or did he call?

I called my mom to ask her matter-of-factly about a few things in our family history. And when I brought up Aunt Leelee, and Trent and Robin, she had trouble remembering some of the details, too.

"Hold on. Let me ask Dad," she said.

And before I could finish saying, "No, no! That's okay. You don't need to—," she put the phone on speaker, and my dad was right there.

I didn't *want* to talk about it, especially with him. We *never* talked about it. After the funeral we just stuffed it all away somewhere.

I assumed asking about the murder would lead to a fight, to something uncomfortable, something awful—but it didn't. I'm so glad my mom got him on the phone, because that was the first time my mom and dad talked to me, and listened to me, about the pain and the hurt that murder caused all of us.

For the very first time, we talked about what they remembered, and I asked them questions I had always been scared to ask them before. I asked Mom what she remembered about how I handled it as a kid. She said that, much like now, when it comes to conflict or hurt in our family, I become the peacemaker. I just wanted to smooth things over and be a "good little girl."

She said other than my paranoia and fear of strangers and bedtime, she couldn't really see any signs of me grieving. She said I was very blank and emotionless about it as a girl. I basically blocked it out.

My parents reminded me that the four of us went to Aunt LeeLee's house at one point after the killing, to help clean it out. As my parents went about emptying closets and moving furniture out onto a truck, my brother and I were told to pick out things that we might want to keep for ourselves, to remember our cousins. The thing I remember most is not wanting anything. I didn't want the toys Robin could no longer play with. I didn't want the clothes that Robin could no longer wear. My parents insisted I take something, and in the end I took some artwork and schoolwork of Robin's. Maybe because it was something she had created, something she had put into the world that she no longer inhabited, something that I feared would get thrown out. Maybe because it was art, which I loved, and which I had only recently given up on. I don't know. But we still have all of that artwork and schoolwork to this day, in a closet at my parents' house.

I didn't hang it up in my room.

I never wanted it to be taken out of the closet. *Ever.*

My brother was so young, he didn't feel the same attachment I did to the items they left behind. He decided he wanted Trent's Lego box, and he was *so excited* to have *so many Legos*. I thought it was awful. I remember that big box vividly, and when we would play at home, I would get so mad if Patrick tried to pull that box out. I hated the smell when he opened the box, because it smelled just like *them.*

I never said anything about it. I just would not play with him if the box was around.

I'm not sure if Patrick ever put two and two together; if he realized that the reason his big sister wouldn't play Legos with him was because of the box, not him.

Like I said, the trauma affected *everything*. Everything changed because of it.

Since that talk with my parents (and the talks we've had since), the suppressed memories of it all have flooded back in. And just talking about them has been healing. Sharing them has been healing. I want people to know. It explains so much about why I am the way I am, and why I react the way I do, and how I've handled other traumas and issues my entire life.

Talking about trauma *matters*. Talking about trauma *heals*.

I suppose one of the biggest takeaways from the whole experience for me was realizing that I had learned an extremely unhealthy but useful defense mechanism: suppressing all memories, thoughts, and feelings of anything bad that ever happened. In my family, I learned that we do not open this feelings box. We do not speak of it. To open it, to me, would be like opening the box of Legos. The smell of it all would be too overwhelming. It was easier to just walk away.

Now that I was in therapy, I realized that it *wasn't* easier. Suppressing everything hurt us. In order to heal, we needed to unlearn that behavior. And we've been working on it.

After a year of self-reflection, and breathing, and writing, I can honestly say I'm a changed woman. I am shocked at how little time it took to really start to change for the better. I was so worried about taking the time I needed, and addressing my past, and so anxious about looking in the mirror, and so scared about not knowing where I was going or what came next—and it turns out that none of those things were nearly as difficult as my anxiety led me to believe.

Don't get me wrong—sometimes things are still tough. I get anxious, I get panicked, I don't handle everything the way I'd like to right in the moment. But I'm learning how to trust myself. My heart. The things I want.

I'm finally learning to love myself the way God loves me.

Today, I'm not as hard on myself as I used to be over the mistakes I make, or anything else. In part that's because I know that whatever happens next, whatever bumpy roads I might go down, I'll be fine. Why? Because look at what I've been through! I made it. Even after all of *that*, I'm still here. I'm still good. And Jesus still loves me.

When I say that phrase, it isn't something I take lightly. It means that Jesus has given me grace. He knows I'm hurting, and He's there for me. And thank God Jesus is there for me, to help me, so maybe I'll stop myself from hurting myself again. While I'm sure I'll mess up plenty again before I learn my lessons for good, I know for sure that I'm listening now. I'm paying attention. I'm trying harder than ever to find my center.

Sometimes it feels like I've swung to the far edges of the spectrum. I've been Miss Perfect, but I've also gone to bed with a guy (or two or three) who didn't love me while I was trying to be "more relatable" to a TV audience. And both ends of the spectrum left me feeling empty. Why? Because at either extreme, I was living for the validation of other people and what *they* wanted me to be.

That just doesn't work out very well. For anybody.

I put myself in a constant cycle of hurt there for a while, but I know now that I don't have to keep doing that. And like I said: If I can make it through these last couple of years, I can make it through anything.

So can *you*.

I'm able to see that now, and be thankful for it, because of my faith *and* because of my therapy. I'm reclaiming my life and becoming my own person. I'm learning and understanding that I already *am* loved, so I don't need to look for my happiness and my joy to come from a man, or from anybody else.

I'm dating again, but it's different now. I'm not letting myself repeat old habits and patterns that used to hurt me. For one, I'm not rushing into anything just because I feel a "spark" with someone. Actually, more times than not, I'm realizing that the spark is something I should run away from.

When your face gets flushed, your stomach drops, your palms start sweating—all that stuff we've been taught from movies and TV shows to think of as love at first sight, or what happens when the right guy comes along—that isn't necessarily a good thing! What I've learned in therapy is that trauma gets stored in the body, and I've had my share of traumatic dating relationships that were not healthy. So, for me, that flushed, heart-racing feeling in some cases isn't the sign of a great romance. It's the body sending trauma signals because it's familiar with the pain of what this sort of a relationship can bring. In my case (and maybe in yours, too), that spark is actually a warning. It's my body telling me that this *isn't* going to be good for me.

Is it crazy that I'm just learning this now? Do other people know this? I don't think so. I think we've all been taught that the spark is something we should embrace.

I'm not saying that spark doesn't equal chemistry in some cases. Chemistry is good! But you have to know yourself, and you have to know the difference. I mean, you can have chemistry with somebody who's wrong for you in every way. You can have chemistry with someone who's married, but that doesn't mean you should go try to date him!

For me, the difference between connecting with somebody and not being able to breathe with somebody is a big deal. Connecting is what matters. Not the false excitement of that rush that can some-times come over me when I first meet someone.

Taking the time to look at my own patterns showed me why I kept falling for the same type of guys—the ones who would ulti-mately wind up hurting me. (Guys like Luke, and Jed, and Tucker, and Brady . . .) It's easy to fall back into what's familiar, even when that familiarity isn't good for you. If I don't want to do that anymore then I *have* to make a conscious decision to try something different; to go for a guy who's not what I see as familiar, and therefore *won't* wind up hurting me. That's not easy to do! Habits are hard to break. Recognizing the spark as something I need to be cautious of rather than a sign of something I should jump right into took me a little while. But I'm so glad to be figuring this stuff out.

I'm seeing that I don't have to *earn* love, because I *am* loved. I'm learning to love myself so that others are free to love the real me. The full me. And that's a very big difference. Maybe most important of all, I know what kind of love I deserve, and I'm not settling for less.

I'm beginning to understand who I am, and to be comfortable in that. To know that I do not have to be validated and recognized by other people. I'm working on getting to a place where I know that I am loved, *always*.

I'm transitioning from "What do you want to be when you grow up?" to the more mature question: "What do you want to *be*?"

I asked myself that question in my journal recently, and I wrote down a long list of answers. Wouldn't you know it? None of them said anything about being somebody's wife or girlfriend. None of them were about being seen, or famous. None of them mentioned be-ing on TV or being an Instagram star, either. They weren't about my career, or my "status," or anything like that.

What I wrote in my journal is this: I want to be "brave, courageous, joyful, empathetic, strong, beautiful, a leader, patient, resilient, accepting, present, hopeful, grateful, gracious, content, determined, motivated, inspired, creative, humble, vulnerable, smart, kind, assertive, genuine, faithful, free, loving/loved, encouraging, independent, dependable, forgiving, self-compassionate, adventurous, silly" . . . and "*enough*."

That's what I want to be. And it's not that I have to be all of these things all at once, or that I have to receive affirmation from others that I'm being these things. Just going through this process, being on this journey, is *proof* that is who I want to be.

Or maybe I should say, "This is who *I am*." Because this is who I *always* was. This is how God created me. I just buried it. I lost parts of it. So all I really need to do is to allow all of me to come to the surface more often; to stop squishing it down while trying to be who everybody else says I should be.

I'm not Hannah B., the beauty queen, the former Bachelorette and winner of *Dancing with the Stars*. I'm Hannah Brown: brave, courageous, joyful, empathetic, strong . . . and, most important, *enough*!

I *am* enough. I am loved. No more, no less. That's all that matters. And to really believe that—well, that's the goal.

Some days I do. Other days, I'm not quite there yet. And that's okay. Because I know it's the journey I'm on now. I know I'll get there.

I'm a little bit better today than I was yesterday, and hopefully tomorrow I'll be a little better than that.

I mean, honestly, if all of our lives are such a mess, then God bless this mess—because the gift of learning life's lessons is all we need in order to grow.

And that's a miracle.

Thanks to everything I've been through, I'm closer than ever to being who I want to be.

I hope you are, too.

ACKNOWLEDGMENTS

I'm grateful to all of the people who supported me in writing this book.

My family—Mom, Dad, Patrick, and Sissy. Y'all have believed in me from day one. Thank you for always encouraging, and never stifling, my dreams. I can always count on y'all to be in my corner cheering me on. I'm so grateful you have allowed me to vulnerably share our family's journey to healing.

Mom—for your selflessness. You live your life to love and support me. You're the OG who helped make this all come true. You've always said I'm the best parts of Dad, but every day, I see more and more of you in me. And I'm happy with that; I just wish I could find my keys.

Dad—for your resilience, and showing me a person can change and grow. I'm so proud of you and love how much we've grown together. I'll always be your baby girl.

Adam, my sweetie—you are my rock (and my scribe because I can't type). Thank you for being my number one fan and loving and embracing me in such a transformational time. You've healed my heart.

The whole team at UTA—thank you for your support, especially Albert Lee, Max Stubblefield, and Jamie Youngentob.

Albert—you believed this could happen when it felt like no one else did. Not even myself. I'll never forget that call letting me know we are getting back to work. Your enthusiasm makes things happen.

Max—for not giving up on me and believing in my renewal. You knew I had something to say. I'm so thankful for your guidance and direction.

Jamie—for always being in the thick of it with me. You have gone above and beyond in so many ways from the very beginning of this whirlwind.

Melissa Fox, Adam, HJTH—bless your hearts. Thank you for protecting and fighting for my story to be told.

Mark Dagostino—thank you for the months, days, and hours and hours and hours spent bringing my story to life. You helped me say the things I've been scared to say. You fully invested in me, even through all of the nit-picking, back-and-forth, spiraling, and rewriting. It seemed like every obstacle tried to slow us down, but we prevailed.

The team at HarperCollins—Anna Montague, Lisa Sharkey, Kate D'Esmond, Katie O'Callaghan, Amelia Beckerman, Maddie Pillari, Cindy Achar, Nikki Baldauf, Nancy Singer, and Caroline Johnson.

Anna—thank you for your patience and guidance. Editing the life of a hot mess can't be easy. God bless you for keeping the train wreck on the tracks.

Lisa—thank you for your diligence and inspiration to get this story into the hands of others. You understood the importance of this undertaking.

Clare Anne, Lena, and the team at Frank PR—thank you for working so hard to make my story heard, I appreciate everything you've done for me.

Lori—I tell you things I wouldn't tell my mother. I was so scared and ashamed to start therapy at first, but because of my experience with you, I *wish* everyone had a therapist! You've been such a big part of this book in helping me dig deeper than I ever would myself. You made me go there to feel and to make sense of all the patterns of hurt . . . and then gave me the tools to heal. Thank you for supporting me and spending hours and hours helping me clearly process the pain and purpose of it all to share with readers.

Ziza—thank you, thank you, thank you. While the circumstances for us coming together were not ideal or pleasant, I am blessed and better for it. Thank you for your knowledge, and your support of my journey.

Lauren Alexandra—for the cover photo and author photo.

Finally, thank you to everyone who read this book. I'm so grateful to have had this opportunity to tell my story, and I can only hope that the people who read it found some of what they needed in the pages.

About the Author

Hannah Brown starred on season 15 of ABC's hit reality series *The Bachelorette*, and went on to win season 28 of *Dancing with the Stars*. The beauty pageant titleholder and winner of Miss Alabama USA 2018 is originally from Tuscaloosa, Alabama. She now lives in Los Angeles, California. You can find her on Instagram, Twitter, and YouTube (@HannahBrown), Facebook (@HannahBrownOfficial), and TikTok (@HannahKBrown).